Institute of Leadership
& Management

superseries

Understanding
Workplace
Information
Systems

FIFTH EDITION

Published for the
Institute of Leadership & Management

ELSEVIER

AMSTERDAM • BOSTON • HEIDELBERG • LONDON • NEW YORK • OXFORD
PARIS • SAN DIEGO • SAN FRANCISCO • SINGAPORE • SYDNEY • TOKYO
Pergamon Flexible Learning is an imprint of Elsevier

Pergamon
Flexible
Learning

Pergamon Flexible Learning is an imprint of Elsevier
Linacre House, Jordan Hill, Oxford OX2 8DP, UK
30 Corporate Drive, Suite 400, Burlington, MA 01803, USA

First edition 1986
Second edition 1991
Third edition 1997
Fourth edition 2003
Fifth edition 2007

Editor: David Pardey

Based on material in previous editions of this work

The views expressed in this work are those of the authors and do
not necessarily reflect those of the Institute of Leadership &
Management or of the publisher

Notice
No responsibility is assumed by the publisher for any injury and/or damage to persons or
property as a matter of products liability, negligence or otherwise, or from any use or operation
of any methods, products, instructions or ideas contained in the material herein

British Library Cataloguing in Publication Data
A catalogue record for this book is available from the British Library

Library of Congress Cataloguing in Publication Data
A catalogue record for this book is available from the Library of Congress

ISBN 978-0-08-046440-4

For information on all Pergamon Flexible Learning publications
visit our website at http://books.elsevier.com

Institute of Leadership & Management
Registered Office
1 Giltspur Street
London
EC1A 9DD
Telephone: 020 7294 2470
www.i-l-m.com
ILM is part of the City & Guilds Group

Typeset by Charon Tec Ltd (A Macmillan Company), Chennai, India
www.charontec.com
Printed and bound in Great Britain

07 08 09 10 11   10 9 8 7 6 5 4 3 2 1

Working together to grow
libraries in developing countries

www.elsevier.com | www.bookaid.org | www.sabre.org

ELSEVIER   BOOK AID International   Sabre Foundation

Contents

Series preface

Whether you are a tutor/trainer or studying management development to further your career, Super Series provides an exciting and flexible resource to help you to achieve your goals. The fifth edition is completely new and up-to-date, and has been structured to perfectly match the Institute of Leadership & Management (ILM)'s new unit-based qualifications for first line managers. It also harmonizes with the 2004 national occupational standards in management and leadership, providing an invaluable resource for S/NVQs at Level 3 in Management.

Super Series is equally valuable for anyone tutoring or studying any management programmes at this level, whether leading to a qualification or not. Individual workbooks also support short programmes, which may be recognized by ILM as Endorsed or Development Awards, or provide the ideal way to undertake CPD activities.

For learners, coping with all the pressures of today's world, Super Series offers you the flexibility to study at your own pace to fit around your professional and other commitments. You don't need a PC or to attend classes at a specific time – choose when and where to study to suit yourself! And you will always have the complete workbook as a quick reference just when you need it.

For tutors/trainers, Super Series provides an invaluable guide to what needs to be covered, and in what depth. It also allows learners who miss occasional sessions to 'catch up' by dipping into the series.

Super Series provides unrivalled support for all those involved in first line management and supervision.

Unit specification

Title:	Understanding workplace information systems	Unit Ref:	M3.34
Level:	3		
Credit value:	I		

Learning outcomes		Assessment criteria		
The learner will		The learner can (in an organization with which the learner is familiar)		
1. Understand the need to maintain information systems	1.1 1.2 1.3 1.4 1.5	Explain the purpose of record keeping for the organization Identify key information to be recorded to meet organizational and legal requirements Identify appropriate systems to store and retrieve information Explain the need to control data access Identify records which are included under relevant legislation (for example the Data Protection Act 1998)		
2. Understand the use and application of IT applications in an organization	2.1 2.2 2.3	Identify different uses or applications of spreadsheets and/or databases in the organization Explain the value of electronic communication methods Describe the back-up system for IT applications in the organization		

Workbook introduction

1 ILM Super Series study links

This workbook addresses the issues of *Understanding Workplace Information Systems*. Should you wish to extend your study to other Super Series workbooks covering related or different subject areas, you will find a comprehensive list at the back of this book.

2 Links to ILM qualifications

This workbook relates to the learning outcomes of M3.34 Understanding workplace information systems from the ILM Level 3 Award, Certificate and Diploma in First Line Management.

3 Workbook objectives

Ever since civilization began, information has been important. In the modern world we are completely dependent on it, and we are creating it in unprecedented volumes.

Commentators often suggest we are simply piling up information pointlessly and one is entitled to wonder whether the 90 or so daily newspapers, 10,000 magazines and 80,000 books published annually in Britain are all worth preserving, let alone the hundreds of thousands of web pages that are newly created every day.

Nevertheless, when it comes to our working lives, the fact is that most of the information we create has a practical value. That means we have to store it and be confident that we can lay our hands on it when we need it.

Systematic approaches to information storage and retrieval are of vital importance in our economy and society. There is so much information that anything that gets misplaced may well be lost forever – a risk that is simply unacceptable.

Over the centuries many people have put their minds to how best to manage the storage of information. Native Americans developed ways of recording stories by patterns of knots in coloured fibres. Australia's Aboriginal inhabitants recorded their own stories and beliefs in ritual paintings. In other parts of the world, people eventually invented writing and created libraries. And some unknown hero must at some point have devised the filing cabinet.

As technologies developed, new systems and approaches appeared and flourished. But the twentieth century is the age of information and now only revolutionary new technologies can cope with our information management needs. Information Technology (IT) – fast, compact and reliable digital electronic systems – has provided an answer. Yet by doing so it has opened the floodgates, and the tide of information is rising like never before.

In this workbook we will start by thinking about manual systems for information storage, including the traditional filing cabinet, folders and index cards. Paper-based systems are still very common in all organizations and many tried and trusted general principles also apply to computerized systems. Most of the workbook will in fact be concerned with the use of computers for storing and retrieving information at work and, in particular, the value of databases. We will also deal with the security of IT equipment and data, and with the law on the storage of personal data on computers.

3.1 Objectives

On completion of this workbook you will be better able to:

- explain the principles behind any system for storing and retrieving information and the key content that organizations are likely to record;
- describe and evaluate the range of data storage media presently available;

- organize the systematic and secure storage of data in manual and computer-based systems;
- identify the use and application of databases and spreadsheets;
- outline the law on data protection.

4 Activity planner

The following Activities need some planning and you may want to look at them now.

- Activity 8, in which you are asked to review and comment on a manual information storage system in your organization.
- Activity 22, which asks you to comment on the rules for file naming in your organization and see how far they are followed by your own work team.
- Activity 36, which calls for a critical review of the data backup policies in your organization.
- Activity 42, where you draw up a policy for your team to ensure that you are complying with the Data Protection Act 1998.
- Activity 43, for which you will need to find out where your department keeps any databases that are registered under the Data Protection Act.

Session A
Record keeping and storage media

1 Introduction

This is the age of information, and vast amounts of it are being collected, processed and stored every minute of every day. In developed countries there are extensive records relating to every single citizen. In the business world information about billions of transactions is stored away. And organizations of all kinds, from schools to courts to research institutes to charities to clubs, store information about an amazing variety of things.

We'll begin this session by thinking about the **need for record keeping** and the **key information** that must or may be recorded by businesses.

The remainder of the session is about the **physical characteristics** of the main types of **storage system** – paper and computer storage. Sessions B and C explore how such systems can be organized in ways that make it easier to **retrieve information**, while Session D looks at the need to **keep records safe.**

2 Why we keep records

Records have been kept ever since the first organizations were set up and the technical means of creating them (i.e. writing) were discovered.

What has changed is the scale of information handling. Over the last 100 years there has been an explosive growth in:

- business activity;
- government activity;
- educational activity;
- military, scientific, legal, sporting and intellectual activity.

All of that means more information is being generated. But why do we keep so much of this information, and why for so long?

Activity 1   5 mins

Think about these six situations in which records are kept, and in each case try to explain briefly why it is done.

Local authorities storing information about who lives where and what kind of houses they live in.

_____

_____

Hospitals storing records of the consultations, investigations and treatment that they provide to their patients.

_____

_____

Businesses keeping records of sales, stock and customer accounts.

_____

_____

Organizations of all kinds keeping personnel records.

_____

_____

Scientific research projects storing 'raw data'.

Governments collecting and recording all kinds of information about their citizens and their activities (for example through the census).

There are two common reasons for keeping records.

- For **practical, operational needs**. For instance, you constantly need to refer to all the correspondence you have with customers and suppliers, just to do your day-to-day job properly. And records save time, too: if your stationery supplier sends you a catalogue you are under no legal obligation to keep it (even if you asked them to send it), but it might be useful to keep it, and it will probably save you time when you place your next order.
- To provide **management information**. Among other things, data about past activities can be analysed for a variety of purposes, for example to:

  - compare actual performance with targets and budgets;
  - discover trends in costs, revenue and productivity;
  - reveal the net value (profitability) of various activities;
  - predict the likely future shape of the organization.

Such information can help people like you make better decisions.

Local and central government bodies collect and store information for essentially the same reasons. They too want information that will help them make better decisions.

2.1 Legal requirements

However, the most important reason for keeping records is because there are **legal obligations** to do so.

In addition to the Limitations Act 1980 (the 'Statute of Limitations') various types of record are covered by specific legislation, such as company law, tax law, contract law, charity law, consumer law, employment law, pensions law, health and safety law, and so on.

The table below shows recommended retention periods for various types of document but, if in doubt, you should always seek advice from your organization's legal department and accounting department.

Document	Recommended Retention
Accounting and banking records	
Ledgers, invoices, etc.	6 years
Cheques and bills of exchange	6 years
Paying-in counterfoils	6 years
Bank statements	6 years
Instructions to banks (for example standing orders)	6 years
Employee records	
Staff personnel records	6 years after employment ends
Personnel records of Senior Executives	Permanently
Job applications (rejected candidates)	Up to 1 year
Time cards and piecework records	6 years
Payroll records	6 years
Expense claims	6 years
Medical records	Permanently
Accident book	Permanently
Insurance	
Correspondence about claims	3 years after claim is settled
Insurance schedules	7 years
Public Liability, Product Liability and Employers Liability policies	Permanently
Contractual and trust agreements	
Simple contracts, e.g. with customers or suppliers	6 years after contract expires
Contracts under seal (for example related to land and buildings)	12 years after contract expires
Trust deeds (for example a mortgage)	Permanently
Statutory returns, records and registers, board meetings	
All statutory registers	Permanently
Notices, circulars and board minutes	Permanently

Activity 2

Do emails sent by or received by businesses need to be kept? Explain your answer.

_____

_____

_____

Email is considered to be the electronic equivalent of a letter. So if the correspondence is the type that would be kept if it were in paper form (for example an email making an offer or communicating acceptance of an offer) then the email should be kept for a certain time (usually six years), under contract and consumer law.

2.2 Organizational requirements

What records are kept by an organization above and beyond legal requirements depends on how it wants to use the information.

For example, consider the maintenance department of a large commercial company. They will be involved in two main kinds of activity:

- planned maintenance following schedules agreed and budgeted in advance;
- unscheduled maintenance, mainly emergency repairs.

Activity 3

The maintenance department is subject to financial control via budgets and the efficiency of its performance is also measured. What records will the department keep?

_____

_____

_____

The first requirement is always to keep a record of what was done, when, and by whom. This might consist of simple statements such as '26th August: repaired leaking air conditioning unit in room 1320'.

These could be kept as a **log or diary** – a simple list of dates and brief descriptions of what was done. However, proper financial controls would call for more detailed records of costs incurred. In this case these will mainly be labour and materials costs. **Job sheets** should show the **time** spent on each job, and any **materials** used or components installed.

These documents will be filled out by hand and transferred to the computer, probably daily.

If the department holds its own stocks of consumable materials, equipment, spare components, etc. it will need its own **stock record** system. This can probably be quite simple.

The performance side calls for a record of how quickly and efficiently the maintenance department did its work. This might also appear on the **job sheet.**

Activity 4

4 mins

What details would you require in order to measure the performance of the maintenance department in dealing with unscheduled maintenance calls?

_____

_____

_____

_____

Repairs are disruptions that halt or impede the work of people in the organization. The maintenance department is there to ensure that these disruptions are minimized. Planned maintenance is designed to prevent them from occurring; unscheduled maintenance is to clear them up quickly when they do.

The managers responsible will want **records** that help them to judge how effective planned maintenance is by measuring the number of emergency maintenance events that occur. They will need to know:

- how rapidly the department responded to emergency maintenance calls;
- how quickly they carried out the repair;
- how effective the repair was.

This means recording time of call, time of response, time taken to make the repair, plus details of any follow-up.

The time information could perhaps be logged separately, or could be added to the **job sheet**, or both. Follow-up details could be added later.

This is just some of the specific information that the maintenance department will record. It will also need to record its performance on planned maintenance to show:

- work done compared with the **plan**;
- cost of work compared with the **budget**.

This example shows what a lot of record keeping needs to be done to manage an activity efficiently: logs, job sheets, stock records, plans and schedules.

Activity 5

3 mins

You probably record lots of data without even noticing. Why?

_____

_____

_____

Assuming you use a computer for most of your work it records all sorts of things without you having to do any more than start a new document and save it. It will automatically keep a record of the date and time the document was first created, the date and time it was last saved, the author of the document, and so on.

You also indirectly record data about many aspects of your life such as your usage of electricity and gas and the telephone, and your bank account and credit card transactions. Just by using such services you record data on a computer somewhere.

3 Paper-based storage media

Even if they now do all of their work on computer most organizations still have a mixture of paper-based record-keeping systems and computer-based systems.

This is partly because older records may still occasionally be useful, even though they are not in computerized form, and partly because paper documents are constantly received from other organizations and they may need to be kept in some way.

For the foreseeable future, therefore, it is important that you are comfortable with both types of system.

Activity 6

Stately & Graceful Ltd, a specialist firm of seed merchants, buys its seeds from about 100 different growers, many of them overseas.

The firm receives a steady flow of letters, brochures, samples, price lists, product deliveries, invoices, etc. from its suppliers. It also generates goods-received notes, test reports and other documents that are filled in manually by its staff.

Think about this small firm's data storage requirements, and from your own knowledge and experience say briefly how you think it might go about storing its records.

_____

_____

_____

_____

Even small firms routinely use computers to produce letters, purchase orders, invoices, stock lists, etc. Stately & Graceful would certainly do so. We would expect such a firm to store these in two separate ways:

■ on the computers, which it uses to generate them;
■ in manual folders as 'hard copy'.

Where manually-generated documents and data arriving from suppliers are concerned, they will be stored manually, in traditional folders.

The firm will also keep various record books or ledgers, including:

- a goods received book;
- a cash book (using traditional double-entry book-keeping);
- a post log, in which outgoing letters and faxes are listed;
- possibly many others, for example for customer/supplier information.

3.1 Storage for retrieval

We store information so that, when necessary, we can retrieve it and use it for some purpose.

Activity 7 · 4 mins

A supplier rang to ask Stately & Graceful Ltd whether they still wanted the consignment of Lewisia seeds that had been unavailable when ordered. 'That was the order you placed in March,' said the caller. 'We wrote back explaining the hold-up, if you remember.'

The odds are that S&G won't remember, so how would S&G identify the correspondence in question, via their manual filing system?

_____

_____

This may seem like a simple question with an obvious answer, but it raises some important issues about the way records are organized.

- Step one is to find the folder for the particular supplier. This should present no difficulty.
- Step two is to locate the particular documents. This may be easy – but it depends on how well the folder is organized.

If documents are just slipped into the folder, they will probably be out of order. If there is a very large number of documents in the folder, it may take time to find the one in question. It is particularly difficult if the caller can't specify the dates or reference numbers that identify the particular documents required.

EXTENSION I
For more on organizing
the modern office, see
Barbara Hemphill's
useful book.

The worst thing that can happen is that the documents have been carelessly put in the wrong folder: they are then in effect lost, though they may 'turn up' eventually.

So if they're going to be useful, filing systems must be properly organized.

- Documents must be kept in the right place.
- They must be kept in the right order.
- There must be a way of identifying each one with certainty, with a unique code number or correspondence reference.

Without an organized system the storage of data and information is possible, but retrieval is not. Imagine what would happen if Stately & Graceful's staff simply threw every document onto a huge pile. Apart from the fire risk, their documents would be safe, but would anyone ever be prepared to search the growing pile for one item in particular?

Activity 8 · 25 mins

In your organization – perhaps even in your own department – there will certainly be at least one large manual information storage system.

Find out in detail how it is used. Here are some suggested things to investigate.

- The system by which documents are stored and retrieved.
- The physical processes involved (note the time and effort required).
- What happens to folders that are no longer in current use.
- How information in the folders is transmitted to other people and departments who might need it.
- Any special security controls over access.

Now comment on the strengths and weaknesses of this system. You might think about cost, convenience, simplicity/complexity, security and bulk, among other issues.

3.2 How many copies?

Going back to the Stately & Graceful case study, you'll remember that we were talking about an order that had been placed, but had not been fulfilled, and so was still pending.

Activity 9

4 mins

This probably happens quite often to any organization, and it would be reasonable to store details in the relevant supplier folder. If this information was stored only in the supplier folder, what might be the drawbacks, and what solution could you suggest?

_____

_____

_____

Perhaps S&G are not very systematic and don't chase up unfulfilled orders, but most organizations would want to do so. However, such chasing up is very difficult if it means combing through every supplier folder (100 of them, remember) at regular intervals. The obvious answer is to make an extra copy of the order document, which will go in a separate folder. This folder will be held by whoever is responsible for placing and chasing orders.

There's also a case for making some further copies of the order. For example:

- accounts will need one against which to match and clear invoices and payments;
- the person or people responsible for checking in deliveries might also need one.

This need for multiple copies of documents is often met by specially printed multi-part sets. These are commonly used in business. Here are some examples:

- purchase orders;
- goods-in notes;
- invoices and bills;
- credit notes;
- statements;
- repair estimates;
- service reports.

Activity 10

15 mins

It's likely that your organization uses multi-part document sets. Choose one that has at least three parts, and trace where they go, what they are used for, and by whom. Note down brief details below.

_____

_____

_____

_____

Multi-part documents are records of a transaction of some kind. The various parts are distributed to the people and departments that need to carry out further processes involving the same information. A goods-in note, for example, may consist of four parts, which are distributed as follows.

■ The 'top copy' is filed by the goods-in department.
■ The second goes to the accounts department, who need to match it to the supplier's invoice before authorizing payment.
■ The third goes to stores, who need it for updating their stock records.
■ A fourth goes to purchasing, to confirm that the order they had placed has been fulfilled.

Activity 11

4 mins

It may have occurred to you that this kind of information processing could be computerized. What advantages might this bring?

_____

_____

_____

_____

_____

_____

Under a manual system, a lot of paper records are constantly moving about, and each department involved is storing its own sets of records. A computerized system in which one centrally stored record is processed and updated as necessary could have many advantages. For example:

■ it removes the need for several separate paper-based filing systems;
■ it reduces the amount of paper in transit;
■ it speeds up the transfer of the information from department to department;
■ it reduces costs.

3.3 The problems with manual information storage

There is no reason why traditional manual information storage systems should not be effective. Small organizations – and small units in bigger ones – may be perfectly happy with their traditional methods. However, there are problems and opportunities in manual data storage systems.

Activity 12

Get hold of a typical A4 hanging file from a cabinet – one from your own department if possible.

First establish some data.

■ How much does it weigh?
■ How much does it cost, together with the bits and pieces needed to hang it in the filing cabinet or rack?
■ How much does a standard four-drawer filing cabinet cost?
■ How many typical files will a standard four-drawer filing cabinet hold?

Now use your data to answer the following questions.

Assume that Stately & Graceful Ltd's 100 supplier files are of the same size as your 'typical' one.

■ How many four-drawer filing cabinets will they need to store them? Assume each drawer is 50 cm deep.
■ How much will the storage facilities cost? Look this up in an office equipment catalogue.
■ How much will the files themselves weigh in total?

Think about the consequences of this for an organization with much larger storage requirements.

See page 102 for our comments on this question.

When information is stored on a large scale by traditional methods, the burdens are significant in terms of:

- capital cost;
- bulk and weight, which may require new premises or stronger floors;
- annual running cost.

That is just the storage side of things, but we also have to consider retrieval. One person can comfortably work with a single filing cabinet. You soon get to know where everything is, and you only have to move a short distance to store or retrieve an item.

With 50 – and sometimes many more – cabinets to cope with it may take years for anyone to get to know the contents thoroughly. Most staff never will; and there comes a point where so many files are kept that no single person could ever keep track of everything. Information overload!

That's not all; the physical task of storing and retrieving data becomes much bigger. In our example of 50 filing cabinets, users would have to move up and down a 23.5 metre row of cabinets. That soaks up time and energy; in effect it means that a specialized team of staff is needed to operate the system, with important implications for costs.

Small-scale data storage systems on traditional manual lines work well. But when they grow they soon become very burdensome, even when they work effectively.

3.4 Making manual data storage more efficient

Some organizations – banks, local government, big companies – may have large numbers of files. There is therefore strong pressure to find ways of reducing the cost of storing and retrieving this paperwork.

Three main approaches have been used: high-density storage; automated systems; and transferring paper documents to a less bulky medium.

High-density storage

Where traditional filing cabinets are used, it is necessary to allow three times the actual 'footprint' of the filing cabinets so that staff can move around them.

This is based on the calculation that when one person has fully opened a filing cabinet drawer another person may still need to get past him or her.

However, it is possible to devise systems whereby the cabinets are packed tightly together, but are mounted on rollers or rails, so that they can be pulled out to a position where they can be accessed. The illustration below shows how this might work for taller and longer storage units.

There are some safety considerations here, especially when the units are power-assisted (as some need to be in view of their great weight).

High-density storage usually involves special systems rather than ordinary filing cabinets, which after all are only some 132 cm tall. There is always space above them that could be used. Sliding and rotating units can hold thousands, rather than hundreds of files, and can bring them down to a convenient position for the operator.

Automated systems

For very large amounts of document filing, fully or semi-automatic systems have been devised. These are similar in principle to advanced warehouse storage systems. Operators can enter a document into the system and tell the machinery in which slot to file it. This is then done automatically, without the operator having to move. The whole file can be retrieved by similar methods.

As you can imagine, such systems are extremely costly and complex; they are a rarity.

Transfer to less bulky media

The build-up of paperwork records causes two problems:

- they occupy too much space;
- accessing them becomes increasingly difficult.

In the 1970s and early 1980s developments in photographic technology provided an alternative – to photograph each document and miniaturize it. This was particularly useful for archiving older files that weren't often accessed; this would leave a smaller and more manageable selection of current files in paper form.

Two approaches were used: microfilm and microfiche.

- **Microfilm**, as its name suggests, is a roll of film with each frame representing a page of a document – or perhaps a two-page spread from a book or report. Microfilm was widely used for archiving newspapers, magazines and scientific journals; it was popular with public libraries for these purposes.
- **Microfiche** is a more rigid rectangular piece of film about the size of a postcard, though formats vary. Each fiche can contain large numbers of micro-images – usually pages of documents. Microfiche was much used to archive records such as bank statements and building society savings records.

Special machines are needed to magnify the micro-images and make them readable. For instance, microfiche readers allow the user to move the fiche around quickly under the viewer to find the right frame(s); more advanced machines can be programmed to access a particular frame automatically.

A further development enabled frames from microfilm or microfiche to be printed out, so that the documents stored could be made available in hard copy again. This, and the realization that film could itself be copied very cheaply, led to a micropublishing boom.

Activity 13

What would you say were the two main disadvantages of microfilm and microfiche as information storage media?

_____

_____

Most organizations would consider that these micromedia had their uses, but there are drawbacks.

■ The process of transferring documents to film is somewhat cumbersome.
■ The information they contain is relatively awkward to access, with special equipment needed.

We might add that even though they take up much less space than hard copy folders and documents, they are still relatively large objects. They also require special systems for storage.

It is most unlikely that you will come across a system that still converts documents to microfilm or microfiche today, but if you find yourself working for a large and long-established organization such as a bank or a building society you may occasionally find that you need to track a topic back to the early 1990s or before, in which case you may well find yourself delving into microfiche.

The modern equivalent of microfilm and microfiche is to create **digital images** of the paper documents and store them on a medium such as **compact disc (CD)**.

4 Electronic storage media

The need for economy, convenience and speed of access has driven the development of electronic systems. Computers have given rise to entirely new ways of storing and retrieving records.

EXTENSION 2
Keep up-to-date with the latest developments in this field through the wide range of publications available.

Data is represented in 'digital' code – the ultra-basic numerical language that computers use for their internal processes. This applies to all kinds of data, from numbers and text to sounds, graphics and video images. Anything that can be digitized can be processed, stored and retrieved by computer.

Digital electronic data storage is extremely attractive because:

■ the storage media have great and rapidly growing storage capacity;
■ they are very compact;
■ the process of storing data is quick and easy;
■ many storage media allow data to be retrieved equally quickly and easily.

4.1 Magnetic and optical media

Media for digital storage can be divided into two broad types.

■ Magnetic storage media, such as a computer's hard disk, floppy disks and tape. The series of digital 1s and 0s are recorded as a magnetic field which is recognized by a read/write device.

Magnetic media are most convenient when you want to be able to erase, rewrite or update the data you have stored.

■ Optical storage media, such as CDs and digital video discs (DVDs). The series of digital 1s and 0s are represented by tiny 'pits' or indentations in a spiral track (much like an old vinyl record) and these pits are recognized when a laser beam bounces light onto the disk.

Some optical storage media can only be written to once (rewritable disks are relatively new at the time of publication, especially in the case of DVDs).

Computer storage capacity is measured in 'bytes'.

■ 1 kilobyte (KB): 1024 bytes;
■ 1 megabyte (MB): 1,048,576 bytes;
■ 1 gigabyte (GB): 1,073,741,824 bytes.

A single page Microsoft Word letter takes up about 20 KB of space but this is because it includes a lot of data that Word needs in addition to the actual text of your letter. If you add a second page you will only increase file size by about 1 KB.

On this very approximate basis a gigabyte represents about 1 million pages.

Activity 14 ·

If a lever arch file holds 500 pages and is 8 cm wide, how many metres of shelving would be needed to hold the same amount of data as a 20 GB hard disk?

_____

_____

The answer is approximately 3,355 metres, or if you prefer about 2 miles!

4.2 Typical storage facilities

Below we set out the features of the most common electronic storage media. This information was up-to-date at the time of publication of this book (Spring 2003), but it may not be by the time you read it. Storage media technology is still developing at an astonishing rate, and the price per megabyte is steadily falling. This is obviously good news, though there is one danger: the more storage capacity we have, the more we will be tempted to fill!

■ **Hard disks**
Typically 20 GB to 40 GB, but hard disks with a capacity of 120 GB are now available for only a relatively small extra cost.

Information retrieval is almost instant because (unlike tapes) disks allow accurate and swift random access to all data stored on them. They are therefore an ideal replacement for the traditional 'random access filing cabinet' – though of course they are hundreds of times smaller.

Removable hard disks are a feature of some laptop/notebook computers, either to increase the overall storage capacity or as a security feature. In networked systems, storage may be provided centrally by computers called file servers, which may have several hard disks each and may be linked to other file servers and storage devices.

■ **Floppy disks**
Although gradually disappearing, these are still widely used. Data storage capacity is up to 1.44 MB, which is perfectly sufficient for a few documents. Data retrieval is slower than it is with a hard disk, but not exceptionally so. Nonetheless, new desktop computers do not come with a floppy disk drive as standard – if you use floppy disks you will need to purchase a separate drive for them. Files that were once sent through the post on floppy disk are now often emailed, zip disks and CDs have largely replaced them for storing large amounts of data. For easy portability many people now use flash drives where once they used floppy disks. These are small, about the size of your thumb, and can store 1 GB or more.

■ **Zip disks**
The best known are Iomega Zip disks with capacities of 150 MB, 250 MB or 750 MB.

Zip drives compress the data for storage purposes and uncompress it when it is needed. The disks they use are much thicker and sturdier than floppy disks.

■ **CD-ROM, CD-R and CD-RW**
CDs can store up to 650 MB of data. All new computers now come fitted with a CD-ROM drive and many have a CD-R or CD-RW drive which enables CDs to be written as well as read.

A CD-R can be written to only once; a CD-RW can in theory be used in much the same way as a floppy disk. In spite of that, most users do not often want to store 650 MB of data temporarily, so CD-Rs are more common.

Retrieval is about as fast as it is for a floppy disk.

- **DVD, DVD-R, DVD-RW and DVD-RAM**
  DVDs are similar to CDs but they have a much larger capacity and may be double-sided. They can hold between 4 and 15 GB of data.

  Rewritable DVDs come in competing formats: DVD+RW, DVD-RW and DVD-RAM. However, multi-format DVD writers are becoming increasingly common, making it possible to read from and write to alternative types of DVD.

  The chances are that rewritable DVDs will become the norm for day-to-day storage during the shelf-life of this book.

- **Tapes**
  Tapes or tape 'streamers' are specially-made high-speed tapes used for backing up large amounts of data held on a hard disk. Tapes can typically hold about 30 GB (or 60 GB in compressed format).

  Tape is not a suitable medium for day-to-day storage and retrieval because data is stored in sequence, just as you might record a TV programme on a videocassette. In order to retrieve a particular part of the data, the tape must be spooled back or forth to the right point. This is perfectly feasible, but it is slow. This is why tapes are generally used only for backup purposes, not as primary storage media.

4.3 Data compression software

There are various methods of compressing computer data and so reducing the size of a computer file, sometimes by up to 90%. If you have smaller files you can of course store more data.

File compression works by finding repeated patterns in data and replacing them with index numbers, which take up much less space. For example, if every occurrence of the word 'the', 'it' and 'a' in this book were replaced by the numbers 1, 2 and 3 it would be a much shorter book.

Compressed files are not, of course, human-readable in their compressed form.

The most widely used formats and compression programs are as follows.

- .zip files – usually created with a program such as PKZip or WinZip. Zip files are very widely used on the Internet to reduce download times.
- .gz files – common on Unix systems, and handled using the Gzip and Gunzip programs, usually built in to Unix systems.
- .sit files – a compression technology for the Apple Mac, created with a program called Stuffit.
- .cab files, much used by Microsoft and others to distribute computer software.

In addition some programs – especially accounting programs – provide their own compression utility and file format. You use this when you want to backup the data produced by the program.

Self-assessment 1

10 mins

1 What is the most important reason for keeping records?

_____

_____

2 Give three examples of records that are kept to help manage an activity efficiently.

_____

_____

_____

3 Why are paper-based storage systems still common?

_____

_____

4 What happens to a paper document that is mistakenly filed in the wrong place?

_____

_____

5   What are the advantages of electronic storage over paper-based storage?

    _____

    _____

6   What electronic storage media would you expect to be used for:

    ■ a multimedia encyclopaedia?

    _____

    ■ backing up the whole of the data held on a computer?

    _____

    ■ a computer's operating system and frequently used applications?

    _____

    Answers to these questions can be found on pages 102–3.

5 Summary

■ Records are kept for a variety of reasons, including:

   ■ to comply with legal requirements;
   ■ to meet operational or financial needs;
   ■ as a source of management information to help with decisions.

■ Whether information is stored manually or electronically, it must be done systematically. Otherwise the information will be impossible to retrieve.

■ In manual systems, some information about transactions may need to be distributed to several different places by means of multi-part sets.

■ Manual information storage systems work well on a small scale. Large ones make excessive demands on money, space and time.

■ Electronic storage is the preferred solution and it has many advantages, including:

   ■ very large storage capacities;
   ■ very compact storage media;
   ■ quick and simple random-access storage and retrieval.

■ Electronic media consist of: magnetic media such as hard disks, floppy disks and tapes; and optical media such as CDs and DVDs.

■ You can get better use out of the available storage space in a computer system by using a data compression program.

Session B
Systems for storing and retrieving information

1 Introduction

These days everyone is on the receiving end of so much information that it's all too easy to lose track of the important bits. The only way to be certain of where to find the information you need is to be systematic about storing it.

That means two things:

- sorting and organizing the information into meaningful categories and being consistent about its content;
- putting it into the right places promptly and regularly.

There are bound to be problems when information is stored in the wrong place, or in the wrong order – or not stored at all. With so much information coming in important items can easily get lost forever.

That's why you need a system, and being systematic starts with the way you sort and organize your information. Unless information is organized in some way its users will not know where it is and how to retrieve it later when it is needed.

The first parts of this session describe the various systems of classification, indexing and cross-referencing commonly found in organizations: much of this applies to both manual and computer systems. The final part describes how you can organize information on your computer and use its search tools to help you find documents.

2 Organizing information

2.1 Terminology

There is a very big difference between computer terminology and paper-storage terminology.

■ In manual systems a 'file' is simply a physical container such as a lever-arch file. The file contains a collection of separate leaves.

The contents may be leaves of paper, or leaves of plastic acetates or similar. Some of the leaves my contain words while others have only pitures. Others will have both. The key thing is that there are separate leaves.

■ In computer systems a 'file' is a collection of data in the same computer format. For instance you can have a '.txt' file containing text or a '.jpg' file containing a picture. (Some computer formats can contain both text and graphics but these can usually only be opened and viewed properly using the computer program that created them. Microsoft Word's '.doc' format is an example.)

To avoid confusion we will use the term 'folder' when we are talking about containers for documents, and 'file' for individual documents.

2.2 Manual systems

In a manual system, paper documents are generally kept in **different folders** for different types of information. Information within an individual folder might be divided again into **categories** and then held in a particular order within each category. If folders are subdivided by topic (customers, employees, and so forth) colour coding is often used to avoid placing information in the right sequence but under the wrong topic.

Activity 15

You have a letter dated 5 August 2003 from Mrs JK Fallone of SDS Interiors Ltd in Barnsley about a contract to redecorate your office. How could this be filed so that it would be easy to retrieve?

_____

_____

_____

There are various ways in which folders can be **classified** and **structured**. Here are some of the many possibilities.

- By **name** – for example letters to a particular person or organization.
- By **subject matter** – for example documents about a particular project, transaction or problem.
- By **date** – all invoices for a particular year, for instance.
- By **geography** – by country, area or city, for example.
- By **department** – for example salary details or personnel records for employees of each department.
- By **product** – everything relating to product A, product B, and so on.
- By **customer type** – for instance corporate clients' data may be kept separate from individual clients' data.

In practice many systems combine two or more methods.

2.3 Information within folders

Once a broad structure has been established, the material within folders can be put into a **sequence**. Again there are various possible systems, including the following.

- **Alphabetical** order – for example suppliers arranged in name order.
- **Numerical** order – for example invoices arranged in order of invoice numbers.
- **Alpha-numerical** (A1, A2, A3, B1, B2, etc.).
- **Chronological** order – for example correspondence is typically arranged in date order with the most recent at the front.

These ways of subdividing and arranging data in a logical way within suitable categories make it possible to store, find and also cross-reference or index information efficiently.

2.4 Alphabetical classification

A very common method of classification is alphabetical: items are filed according to the first and then each successive letter of a person's last name or a company's full name. This is usually straightforward, but there are some conventions that you should be aware of.

Surnames	
The hyphen is ignored in double-barrelled names. When surnames are the same, initials or first names are taken into account.	Gage Gaines Gainsborough Gale Gale-Brown Gales Gallagher, Anthony Gallagher, Christine
Initials	
Names made up of initials come before whole-word names.	RJK Ltd Rabelais Ltd
Prefixes	
Prefixes are included as part of the surname.	De Havilland Le Grande Von Dewitz
Mc/Mac and St/Saint	
Mc is treated as if it were 'Mac' and St is treated as 'Saint'	Maby McAdam Macalister McArthur Sainsbury St John Saint Mary's Church
Titles and common words	
Words like 'Mr', 'Mrs', 'Sir', 'The', 'A' are ignored for filing purposes. Systems vary with regard to institutions like departments and universities.	Department of Fair Trading Ealing, University of Wandsworth, London Borough of
Businesses	
Businesses with names like 'Philip Archer & Son', 'Frank Aston Ltd', are sometimes listed under the first letter of the surname (as if they were ordinary names) but it is more usual to put them under the first letter of the whole name.	Frank Aston Ltd Philip Archer & Son
Numbers	
Numbers at the beginning of names usually appear before any names beginning with A, in numerical order, with any initial 0s ignored.	5 Star Ltd 6 S Communications 6a Ltd 007 Car Services

You will find things arranged differently in some cases. For instance in some systems numbers are treated as if they were spelled out as words, so you might find '3D Digital Design' under 'T'.

Activity 16

Rules vary from system to system. If you are not already familiar with them you should get to know the ones you have to work with in your organization.

2.5 Chronological classification

A chronological system arranges information by date, usually with the oldest document at the back. Correspondence is usually filed in this way.

2.6 Numerical classification

Numerical sequence

Numerical sequence is appropriate for standard pre-printed documents. For instance, invoices are numbered, so if you need to check one you just have to know the number (this may be given to you by the person making the enquiry or you may be able to look it up in the customer's account).

Numerical sequence is more flexible than the alphabetical method in a manual system. For instance, you do not have to decide in advance how much space to allocate to each letter, so you do not have to shuffle all the documents about if you allow too little space for the letter T, say. With numerical order, you simply give a new document the next number and position in the system.

On the other hand, numbers may not be very meaningful on their own: 'invoice 392481' does not tell you anything about what the invoice was for.

Numerical subject systems

Numbers can be given a meaning to a limited extent. For instance, a building society might have account numbers constructed from three parts. A number in the form 4–839–20451 would indicate the following.

- It is a type 4 account (which allows instant withdrawal and pays 4.25% interest, say).
- The account was opened at branch 839, and branches in the 800–899 range are in the South West region.
- It is account number 20451 opened at that branch, and that number can be identified with a specific customer.

Obviously you will need some kind of index to make a numerical-subject classification understandable. In this case, you need an index of account types and an index of branches. Individual account numbers will probably be part of the accounting system. We'll talk about indexes and indexing in more detail a little later in this session.

Libraries use the Dewey Decimal Classification system to classify their books in this style. Here are the ten broad categories used in all UK public libraries and many other libraries throughout the world.

000	Computers, information, & general reference
100	Philosophy & psychology
200	Religion
300	Social sciences
400	Language
500	Science
600	Technology
700	Arts & recreation
800	Literature
900	History & geography

Each major group (for example 600 to 699) is further and further broken down. Here's a more detailed extract focusing on the 658 categories, which are devoted to general management issues.

640	Home & family management
650	Management & auxiliary services
651	Office services
652	Processes of written communication
653	Shorthand
654	[Unassigned]
655	[Unassigned]
656	[Unassigned]
657	Accounting
658	General management
658. 1	Organization and finance
658. 2	Management of plants
658. 3 1	Elements of personnel administration
658. 3 1 1	Recruitment and selection of personnel
658. 3 1 1 1	Recruitment
658. 3 1 1 2	Selection

658.	4	Principles of management
658.	5	Management of production
658.	6	[Unassigned]
658.	7	Management of distribution (Marketing)
658.	8	Management of distribution (Marketing)
658.	9	Management of specific kinds of enterprises

659	Advertising & public relations
660	Chemical engineering

(Note this is only an extract, with many lines omitted. For instance books on management training are classified under 658.3124.)

Activity 17
5 mins

Armed with this information have a wander around the non-fiction section of your local library looking at the codes on the spines of the books. The arrangement of the whole library should suddenly make much more sense to you!

Again, indexes or catalogues are needed to make the system workable.

- If you want to find a particular book, you look up the title or author in an alphabetical index to get the Dewey reference number.
- If you want a book on a certain subject, you use an index or catalogue which lists the range of numbers you should be looking in: you can then find relevant books on the shelves devoted to that range.

A system like this is very flexible – extra subdivisions can be added as needed.

Alpha-numeric classification

In an alpha-numeric system, folders are given a reference consisting of letters and numbers. For example a letter received from a Mr Harris about an insurance claim might be given the reference HAR/4129/03/1.

HAR   The first three letters of the correspondent's name.

4129   A number to distinguish this correspondent from anybody else whose names begin Har.

03   This indicates that the correspondence began in 2003.

1   The I shows that it is the first folder that has anything to do with this subject. If Mr Harris makes a separate claim later in the year, the correspondence relating to this would be kept in a separate but related folder HAR/4129/03/2.

A system like this is most useful where there is a very large volume of correspondence on different but related topics.

2.7 Subject classification

Subject classification may be useful when dealing with large contracts, or specific products, or when you want to keep track of a project from beginning to end.

There may be various options for organizing documents within a subject folder and it may be difficult to choose suitable subject headings without overlapping (or leaving too many bits of information under 'miscellaneous'!).

2.8 Geographical classification

Geographical classification is useful for businesses that are organized by region.

The main drawback is that it requires knowledge of geography. This makes it more open to error than alphabetical systems. If you were looking for a document from the Munich office, you would probably know that it was kept in the Germany folder, but if you had to find one from a customer in Nether Wallop, you might have to consult a map to find out which regional folder to look in.

Once folders have been divided into geographical groupings, items within each regional folder are filed in alphabetical order, chronological order or whatever is most appropriate.

 # 3 Cross-referencing and indexing

No matter what structure you choose for your storage system, there will always be items that could be filed in more than one place, or are relevant to more than one aspect of your work.

An easy solution, if a document refers to more than one topic, is to place a copy in each of the relevant folders.

This is a bit of a waste of space though, and sometimes it is not that simple. For instance, classification by **subject** may be a logical way of keeping together all the paperwork for a project. But there will still be gaps and overlaps in folders because of the number of **different people** involved – consultants, suppliers, lawyers, customers – and **other possible 'subjects'** – materials, personnel, regional differences and so on – that may be part of any project. As a result:

- correspondence with a customer or supplier would appear in the folder for each contract concerned;
- there might also be a 'personal' folder for each customer or supplier, to cover all their other dealings with the company, not necessarily specific to any one contract;
- there might be another folder to cover the particular product involved in the contract, since the organization is likely to buy from or sell to more than one supplier or customer.

This is where **cross-referencing** is useful. At the front of each folder you could insert a sheet showing links to other relevant folders: the contract folder would contain a list of all customers/suppliers; their personal folders would contain a list of the contracts they had been involved in.

Activity 18

4 mins

Daspro Limited is a company that makes various items of factory equipment.

Over the years it has completed several contracts for computerized lathes and hydraulic presses for (among other companies) *NQV* Systems plc.

There has also been additional correspondence with Mr S Dumali, *NQV*'s Chairman, on matters generally connected with the business relationship.

In the list below complete the cross-reference column using the folder numbers given. For instance if you think folder 5 should cross-refer to folders 1 and 7 write in 1, 7.

	Folder	Cross reference(s)
1	Hydraulic presses (production, sales etc.)	See also folder(s):
2	Computerized lathes (production, sales etc.)	See also folder(s):
3	NQV Systems plc – Hydraulic press contract (3/2004)	See also folder(s):
4	NQV Systems plc – Computerized lathe contract (8/2002)	See also folder(s):
5	NQV Systems plc – Computerized lathe contract (3/2006)	See also folder(s):
6	Dumali, S – correspondence	See also folder(s):
7	Another Company Ltd – Hydraulic press contract (6/2005)	See also folder(s):

Our answer to this Activity can be found on pages 106–7.

A letter from Mr Dumali about maintenance services (for which there is currently no subject folder) would go into 6, while a letter from Mr Dumali about the hydraulic presses in general and the most recent computerized lathe contract would probably be duplicated and placed in folders 3 and 5.

In real life the numbers 1 to 7 would actually be some kind of code, depending on the organization's coding system.

3.1 Indexing

The manual filing systems we have looked at so far fall into two main types.

- If information is filed alphabetically according to name, subject or geography you should be able to retrieve a document simply because you know the system, without having to look at a separate index.
- If information has been given a numerical or alpha-numerical reference code and put in numerical order you will have to consult a separate index before attempting to find your folder.

Activity 19

Suppose you had 10,000 books and folders and, to make maximum use of limited space, you stored them on shelves according to how big they were.

If you simply numbered them from 1 to 10,000 how would you remember what number you had given to the particular one you wanted to look at?

_____

_____

You would have to record the numbers in an index, which would give you a reasonable idea of where you could find the information you needed. The book titles or authors and the topics of the folders would be listed in alphabetical order as follows.

Title	Code
Active Server Pages	386
Apache: The definitive guide	173

An index can also be a record in itself, sometimes containing enough information to make it unnecessary to consult the folder or document itself.

At some time in your education you may have been taught to create revision cards as an index to your studies. These might have contained a brief summary of the topic as well as references to appropriate pages of your notes and to other index cards on related subjects.

Likewise personnel record cards give basic details on each member of staff, as well as reference to a folder which contains the full information.

If a manual system is used for indexing folders, it needs to cater for insertion or removal of items without disturbing the order, and preferably without leaving gaps.

A **page index** is the system you find in an address book: one or more blank pages are allotted for each letter of the alphabet.

A **card index** consists of small cards which can be written on and stored one behind another in some kind of box or drawer. The best known example of a card index system is the Rolodex card holder.

In a modern system, of course, the index would almost certainly be in computerized form – perhaps a database – but you may well find that card indexes or similar are still in use for older archived documents.

 # 4 Computer systems

Many of the principles that apply to manual systems are just as valid for computer systems: you can organize folders and sub-folders by subject type, by geographical region, and so on. A computer takes some of the hard work out of storage and retrieval, but it is still important to develop good habits and to be careful, especially about keeping copies (backups) of your work.

4.1 Computer file managers

Computers organize documents firstly by the 'drive' on which they are stored (for example, the hard disk drive or the floppy disk drive) and the drive is divided into folders and sub-folders. This is equivalent to a room (the drive), containing filing cabinets (the folders), which contain lever-arch files (sub-folders) in manual systems.

With a computer the number of folders and sub-folders is only limited by the size of the storage medium.

We limit our illustrations in this section to Microsoft. Windows, but Apple operating systems and Unix graphical user interfaces such as Gnome and KDE work in almost exactly the same way.

Windows Explorer and Windows My Computer are more or less the same program. Windows Explore is the one we are using here.

For instance, the folders and sub-folders on the hard disk of a computer owned by Daspro Ltd (see Activity 18) might look like this in Windows Explorer.

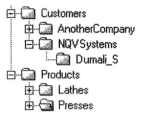

File management programs such as Windows Explorer allow you to sort folders, and the files within folders, according to four criteria: the name of the file; its size in bytes; the type of file; and the date and time last modified.

The list in the following illustration is ordered in alphabetical order of file name. Notice that it is a sort of 'index'.

Name △	Size	Type	Modified
backup.doc	24 KB	Microsoft Word Document	17/08/2002 20:28
Dent_Pres.ppt	37 KB	Microsoft PowerPoint Presentation	14/08/2002 17:32
Dent1.doc	1 KB	Microsoft Word Document	20/08/2002 20:25
Dent10.doc	5 KB	Microsoft Word Document	16/08/2002 08:49
Dent11.doc	38 KB	Microsoft Word Document	20/08/2002 18:17
Dent2.doc	10 KB	Microsoft Word Document	19/08/2002 16:48
DentPres.htm	35 KB	HTML Document	19/08/2002 08:59
DentSales.xls	1 KB	Microsoft Excel Worksheet	18/08/2002 17:08
Doc1.doc	2 KB	Microsoft Word Document	18/08/2002 00:10
flowchart.jpg	1 KB	JPG File	18/08/2002 00:04
Gale.doc	13 KB	Microsoft Word Document	17/08/2002 21:14
Gale-Brown.doc	5 KB	Microsoft Word Document	14/08/2002 17:32
Gales.doc	5 KB	Microsoft Word Document	28/08/2002 10:06
HAR_4129_03_1.doc	2 KB	Microsoft Word Document	17/08/2002 20:22
logo.gif	24 KB	GIF Image	16/08/2002 16:02
Maternity.doc	38 KB	Microsoft Word Document	20/08/2002 18:21
sales.xls	39 KB	Microsoft Excel Worksheet	16/08/2002 08:49
This file name is too long to be...	5 KB	Text File	17/08/2002 20:32
UPPER.doc	8 KB	Microsoft Word Document	28/08/2002 10:05

With a computer you can sort and resort in ascending or descending order simply by clicking on the column title.

For instance here is the previous list reorganized by file type – indicated by the extension, .gif, .htm, etc. – simply by clicking on the Type column heading.

Name	Size	Type △	Modified
logo.gif	24 KB	GIF Image	16/08/2002 16:02
DentPres.htm	35 KB	HTML Document	19/08/2002 08:59
flowchart.jpg	1 KB	JPG File	18/08/2002 00:04
DentSales.xls	1 KB	Microsoft Excel Worksheet	18/08/2002 17:08
sales.xls	39 KB	Microsoft Excel Worksheet	16/08/2002 08:49
Dent_Pres.ppt	37 KB	Microsoft PowerPoint Presentation	14/08/2002 17:32
backup.doc	24 KB	Microsoft Word Document	17/08/2002 20:28
Dent1.doc	1 KB	Microsoft Word Document	20/08/2002 20:25
Dent10.doc	5 KB	Microsoft Word Document	16/08/2002 08:49
Dent11.doc	38 KB	Microsoft Word Document	20/08/2002 18:17
Dent2.doc	10 KB	Microsoft Word Document	19/08/2002 16:48
Doc1.doc	2 KB	Microsoft Word Document	18/08/2002 00:10
Gale.doc	13 KB	Microsoft Word Document	17/08/2002 21:14
Gale-Brown.doc	5 KB	Microsoft Word Document	14/08/2002 17:32
Gales.doc	5 KB	Microsoft Word Document	28/08/2002 10:06
HAR_4129_03_1.doc	2 KB	Microsoft Word Document	17/08/2002 20:22
Maternity.doc	38 KB	Microsoft Word Document	20/08/2002 18:21
UPPER.doc	8 KB	Microsoft Word Document	28/08/2002 10:05
This file name is too long to be...	5 KB	Text File	17/08/2002 20:32

Activity 20

5 mins

Before you read on, study the illustrations above and comment on how far the order of items follows the rules and conventions given earlier in this session for manual systems.

You may also like to check how the files are ordered in one of the folders on your own computer.

_____

_____

_____

On a computer, file names are sorted in very strict alphabetical order (capitals are treated as lower-case letters), so some of the rules we gave earlier for manual sorting don't apply. For instance, a file named StJohn.doc will appear in the list with other files with names beginning with the letters 'ST' not with other files beginning with 'SA'.

On the other hand a useful trick, if you want a file to appear at the top of an alphabetically sorted list on a computer, is to put an exclamation mark at the front. For instance, a file named '!zzz.doc' will appear at the top of a list of files that also include file names such as 'aaa1111_Plumbers.doc' because the exclamation mark comes first in the computer 'alphabet'.

If you are creating a series of files and you choose to give them the same name with sequential numbers you need to be aware that, when sorted, 'file_10.doc' will appear immediately after 'file_1.doc', not – as you might expect – after 'file_9.doc'. To avoid this add a nought before single digit file numbers: 'file_01.doc' (or if you are creating hundreds of files like this you will need to add two noughts: 'file_001.doc').

Activity 21

3 mins

How are documents typically organized in an email system?

_____

_____

_____

Our answer to this question can be found on page 107.

Certain characters are not allowed in file names. This varies a little depending on the system you are using, but the following rules will serve you well.

The following characters are not allowed in file names or are restricted (the system will simply refuse to save the file if you use one of these in the name).

/   Forward slash
\   Back slash
| Vertical stroke
?   Question mark
<   Less than or left angle bracket
>   More than or right angle bracket

The following characters should be used with care.

Space   Spaces are allowed but are generally best avoided. If you want to separate two words in a file name separate them with the underscore character (e.g. 'my_file').

.   Usually only one full stop is used, to separate the document name from its extension, which usually indicates the format of the document.

"   Double inverted commas are not allowed within the name. If you put them at the beginning and end of the file name but before the extension they will be ignored. If you save a Word document as, say, 'my_file.txt' you will indeed end up with the file my_file.txt: in other words the Word extension .doc will not be used.

~   The tilde is allowed, but note that the system also uses this at the beginning of a file name to indicate a temporary file.

Maximum file name length depends partly which system you are using and partly where you are saving the file. You may find that you can save a file with a name of up to about 250 characters if you save it directly to the 'C' drive, but if you save it in a sub-folder you also have to take account of the number of characters in the name of the sub-folder.

File names longer than about 20 characters are not recommended in any case because:

■ they are difficult to read and take in at a glance;
■ they are not acceptable to some types of compression or backup technology or to saving in certain formats, such as CD-ROM.

Older systems (DOS and Windows 3.1) were far more restrictive about file names: only eight characters were allowed, plus three for the file extension. You may still come across some programs that make you stick to the DOS rules and though it sounds restrictive it does make you take a lot of care with your file naming.

In general you should follow the system of file naming prescribed by your organization if there is one. If not, try to give the file a name that would enable someone else to find it quickly.

Activity 22

Are there any rules for computer file naming in your organization? What efforts are made to ensure that people stick to the rules?

Ask members of your team about their computer file-naming practices and make a note of any problems you identify and any action that you could recommend.

If there are no rules, you could draw up a set of rules for recommendation to your manager – but only after discussion with your team members. It is probably best not to recommend renaming old files if everyone already knows where to find them under the system currently in use.

File size

File size is usually rounded up to the nearest KB or MB. Sorting by file size can sometimes be a useful way of locating a file if you have forgotten its name but remember that it was a 20-page report, not a 1-page letter.

File type

File type is indicated by the file's extension: .doc for a Word document; .xls for an Excel spreadsheet; .htm or .html for a web page; and so on. The extension is usually added by the application that you used to create the file. You will quickly get familiar with the ones you use most often.

Notice that Windows sorts in alphabetical order of its own name for the type of document, not in alphabetical order of file extension. So xls files appear above doc files because 'Microsoft Excel' comes before 'Microsoft Word' when alphabetically sorted.

Again, sorting in ascending or descending order of file type is a useful way of locating a document if you know, for instance, that it is a graphic (for example a .gif or a .jpg file), but can't remember its name.

If you rename a file and alter its file type you will probably get a warning telling you that the application that created the file may not be able to recognize it.

Date modified

This speaks for itself. If you know that a matter was dealt with in June 2002, say, just click on the Modified column and sort the files in ascending or descending date order.

Activity 23 4 mins

Dela wrote a letter to a Mr Sargeant, who had called to complain about Product X, and saved it as 'grumpy.doc'. She did not make a paper copy of the letter apart from the one she posted to Mr Sargeant.

You are now dealing with a further call from Mr Sargeant, who wants to discuss Dela's reply. Dela is on holiday.

How could you find a copy of the letter on Dela's computer?

What advice would you give to Dela for the future?

_____

_____

_____

_____

_____

Your search options depend on the information provided when the document was created and saved. If you create a file in Microsoft Word, for example, there are options (under File … Properties) to give it not just a file name, but also other summary details such as a **subject**, **author name**, **category** and **keywords**. As we will see in a moment, the computer will then be able to search for all files that fit any of these criteria: all files with the subject 'customers', for example, or all files that fall into the category 'complaints' or include the keyword 'Product X'.

In Dela's case it seems unlikely that she bothered with extra file properties. If you can work out where Dela normally saves her letters the best bet initially is to find out the **date** of the letter to Mr Sargeant (ask him) and sort Dela's files in date order. This may restrict the search to just a few documents, but you will still need to look through several files before you find the one you want.

In future, Dela must be encouraged to think of others and use a clearer system. If the file had been given the name 'sargeant.doc' and saved in a folder called 'complaints' this would give another person a reasonable chance of locating the file fairly quickly. Dela could also be encouraged to use the 'subject', 'category' and 'keyword' options.

4.2 Computer searching

No matter how careful and well organized you are, every now and then you will forget where you saved a file or what its name was. Fortunately computers have built-in tools to help you.

- If you were working on it very recently you may find that the application you used has a 'recent file list' under the File menu listing the most recently created files.
- You can use the application's own search facility if it has one. For instance in Microsoft Word if you click on File ... Open and then choose Advanced you get a dialogue box like this.

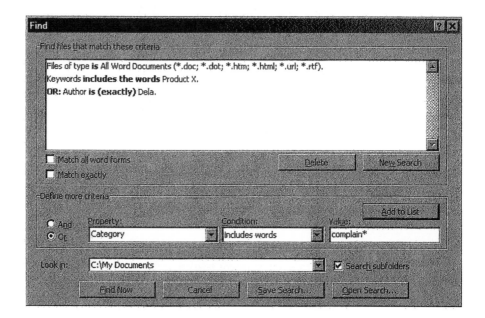

- You can use the system's search facility. In Windows you access this by clicking on Start ... Search ... For Files or Folders. The dialogue box shown in the next illustration shows you what will appear on the screen.

  - You can search either for a specific file name or for files containing specific text or both.
  - You can restrict your search to specific folders. You may know, for instance, that your file is somewhere in a folder called Work_in_Progress: it is much better and quicker to search only the few megabytes of files in this folder than to search the whole 40 GB of your computer's hard drive!
  - You can restrict your search to specific time periods or file types or file sizes.
  - You can ensure that sub-folders are searched as well as the main folder (recommended).
  - You can make your search case-sensitive (not recommended).

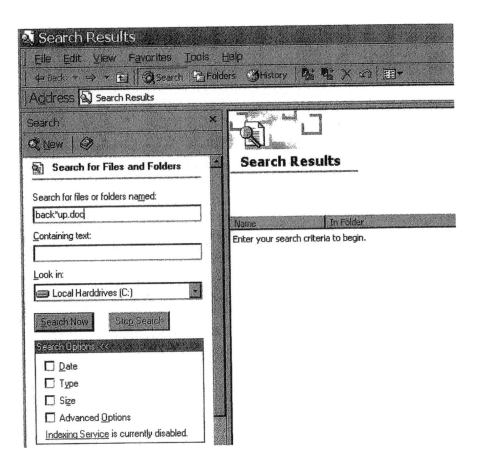

4.3 Wildcards

A wildcard is a character that you can use to represent one or more real characters when you are searching for files or folders. Wildcard characters can be used when you don't know what the real character is or you don't want to type the entire name.

There are two wildcard characters that you can use with a Windows search: the asterisk (*) and the question mark (?).

■ **Asterisk (*)**

You can use the asterisk as a substitute for zero or more characters. If you're looking for a file that you know starts with 'demo' but you can't remember whether it was just 'demo' or whether it had a longer name, type the following:

demo*

A Windows search will locate all files of any file type that begin with 'demo' including demo.ppt, Demonstration.txt, demos.doc, and demo005.doc. To narrow the search to a specific type of file, type the following:

demo*.doc

In this case, the search will find all files that begin with 'demo' but have the file extension .doc, such as demos.doc and demo005.doc, but not demo.ppt or Demonstration.txt.

■ **Question mark (?)**

You can use the question mark as a substitute for a single character in a name. For example, if you typed demo?.doc, the Find dialog box would locate the file demos.doc but not demo005.doc.

You can also use wildcards in the 'Containing text:' box, so if you had written a series of letters in Word to 'ABC Ltd', sometimes spelt 'ABC Limited', and saved them in different places you could locate them all by searching for files named *.doc containing text ABC L*.

Wildcards are useful but take a little care and you should try to be as specific as you can. For instance, if you search for all files containing text *er* that would probably include every file on your computer.

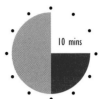

Self-assessment 2

10 mins

1   Fill in the gaps using the words listed below.

Being systematic about the storage of information means the following.

■ Having safe places _____ _____ _____.

■ Sorting and organizing the information _____ _____ _____.

■ Putting it into the right places _____ and _____.

■ Being consistent about its _____ and _____.

CATEGORIES	CONTENT	FORMAT	INTO
IT	MEANINGFUL	PROMPTLY	REGULARLY
STORE	TO		

2   List seven ways of classifying folders.

_____

_____

_____

_____

_____

_____

_____

3   You have paper documents from the following people or organizations. Arrange them in alphabetical order by putting the appropriate number in each box.

Harris-Lane	London Electricity	Albert McLean	Firth, Dr G
1st Class Cleaners Ltd	Messrs Burr Martin & Co	Harrish	London, Jack
Macey, Roger	Anna Maclean	AAA Builders Ltd	HM Customs and Excise

_____

_____

4   There are certain drawbacks to organizing folders by subject, by geography or in simple numerical order. What are they?

_____

_____

_____

_____

5   Which of the following are valid names for computer files? Circle your choice/s.

- HAR/4129/03/2.doc
- Geoff's spreadsheet.xls
- unknown??.doc
- !!index.doc

6   What is the difference between the asterisk wildcard and the question mark wildcard?

_____

_____

Answers to these questions can be found on pages 103–4.

5 Summary

■ Storing information so that it is easy to retrieve means:

- sorting and organizing the information into meaningful categories and being consistent about its content;
- putting it into the right places promptly and regularly.

■ Folders can be organized in various ways, for example by name, by date, or by geographical region. Information within folders will be further organized, usually alphabetically, numerically, or chronologically.

■ Indexing is useful, especially when there is a numerical element in the system of categorization. Cross-referencing may be necessary if documents could be filed in more than one place.

■ Computers take some of the hard work out of storage and retrieval, but it is still important to develop good habits.

■ Careful sorting of files into a file manager and computer search tools can come to the rescue if you forget where you saved a file or what name you gave it.

Session C
Databases and spreadsheets

1 Introduction

There's a good chance that you use some kind of database in your work daily, perhaps without even realizing that you are doing so.

Most modern systems of any size, such as accounting systems, payroll systems, customer relationship management systems, personnel systems and so on, have a database underneath them, although all you ever see is the front-end: some user-friendly computer application that enables you to enter new data and extract reports as and when you wish.

You will also have experienced a database if you use the Internet a lot. If you've searched for a book using Amazon or bought a Christmas present online from Argos, say, you will have explored those companies' databases of products.

This session explains why databases are so useful for storing and retrieving information and how they are often used in businesses.

Database design is a highly skilled and complex art, and good database packages are not usually available as part of the standard 'Office' software, so we can't go into that topic too deeply. However, Activity 28 will teach you some of the basics (you should be able to do this with the software you have on hand) and the other Activities will give you ideas about how you and your work team could benefit from a database.

2 Records and databases

2.1 Records

In computer terms a record is a group of data items that belong together and are stored together in a database. Usually they refer to a particular event or activity such as a job, a purchase, an enquiry, etc.

Activity 24 · 4 mins

Every time you buy something using a credit or debit card, a data record of the transaction is created. Next time you go shopping take a look at one of the till slips (not the credit card voucher) and list the data it contains.

_____

_____

_____

_____

_____

_____

_____

Transaction record slips may vary a bit, but typically they list the time and date of the transaction, the retailer's name and address, the card type, the card number, the authorization code, and the total sum paid. Some slips may list the individual items sold by name, code and price.

Such data records are needed for two main reasons.

- They meet **operational** needs.

  - If there is a query about a transaction, it may be necessary to check it.
  - 'Live' records, such as customer accounts or stock records are used repeatedly and need updating regularly.

- They meet **management information needs**.

  - They can be used to answer the questions that help managers make better decisions about what the organization does and how it can improve.

2.2 Databases

> A database is a collection of records arranged to allow quick and easy identification of specific information.

Where computerized records are stored in a consistent form they are referred to as databases. These are specifically designed to allow quick and easy identification and retrieval of each particular record, but they can do much more than this. Database software, and the way individual records are structured, allow the data to be examined and analysed in many different ways.

For example, suppose a charity creates a simple database for donations. It contains names and addresses of donors, dates and amounts given. The charity can do all sorts of things with this data. It can:

> EXTENSION 3
> Specialist software is available for complex databases. This extension gives guidance on using one such program, Microsoft Access.

- use the dates data to show how many donations were made on a particular day, or in a particular week or month;
- use the address data to show how many donations were made from particular postal areas, counties, etc.;
- use the amounts data to show how the total sums given vary over time by area;
- work out the average amount per donation, over time and by region.

Activity 25   4 mins

Why might it be valuable to a charity to be able to perform this kind of analysis on its database?

_____

_____

_____

Most charities are financially dependent on donations from the public, so they need to know how and why the pattern of donations varies. Analysis of the database can answer all sorts of questions, such as the following.

- What was the response to our last appeal?
- What are the best regions to concentrate on?
- Should we concentrate our appeals at particular times of the year?
- What is the overall trend in donations?
- What pattern of donations can we expect next year?

This is information: it answers important questions that managers need to plan and improve the organization for the future.

Now let's consider a typical commercial sales database, which contains records that are primarily there for operational purposes.

Activity 26 · 4 mins

Ramblin & Packer Ltd (travel agents) specialize in holidays for walkers. They accept bookings by post, in person at their offices, or over the telephone. All bookings are computerized and the record is stored.

The record is part of a wider system, and the data items in it trigger certain key activities elsewhere. These include the issue of booking details to airlines, hotels etc., and the issue to the customer of confirmation of booking, invoice or receipt tickets, and follow-up letters.

If the customer subsequently wants to change some detail of the booking, the record is retrieved and updated.

In the case of Ramblin & Packer, this record of a customer's purchase might have other uses. Try to think of two or three.

_____

_____

_____

The most obvious use is for management and financial information. The company needs to know how much money it is taking so that it can manage its cash flow and long-term funding. It also needs to collect this information in order to draw up the statutory financial statements that form part of its annual report and accounts.

For management purposes, it would be useful to know about matters such as:

- when bookings were made;
- the geographical spread;
- where customers saw the company's products advertised;
- what product packages and 'extras' are most and least popular.

However, there is more to be got from a database of customer transaction records, because you learn some interesting things about your customers, including:

- the name and address of someone who has bought a product from you;
- you know how much they were able to or chose to spend;
- you know what kind of holiday product appeals to this kind of person.

EXTENSION 4
Information and guidance about the *Data Protection Act* is available on a website.

That has a value for marketing purposes. The company is able to create a mailing list of ex-customers, who are more likely to buy another holiday from it than the average person. It makes sense to mail offers to these people – perhaps even to enrol them automatically in some kind of club or newsletter, which helps maintain a friendly connection with them.

If the mailing list is large and attractive enough, it may be possible to sell it to other companies who want to market related, but non-competing, products to these particular customers – walking gear, for instance. Sale of mailing lists may be subject to restrictions under the Data Protection Act.

3 Using a database

As we saw in Session B, a computer's file management features enable users to store all kinds of files in a logical way so that they can be retrieved when needed. This resembles a traditional paper filing system.

3.1 Examples of databases

A database is a different proposition: it is an organized collection of items of information that have a common theme and are presented in a similar format. Databases are more like lists, directories or card indexes than filing systems.

Activity 27 · 4 mins

Databases are not necessarily computerized. A telephone directory is a good example of a database. It consists of thousands of similar entries, organized alphabetically and presented in a particular order:

■ surname, initials, address, phone number.

What other databases can you identify, at home or at work?

_____

_____

_____

_____

_____

Many collections of information can be considered to be databases. Here are some examples.

A TV guide	A dictionary
A recipe book	A directory of learning materials
A hotel guide	A mail-order catalogue
An internal telephone directory	An encyclopaedia of music
The membership list of a society	A holiday brochure
A used car price guide	A personal address and telephone book

If you look closely at any such example, you will notice some common features.

■ The database consists of a series of separate entries.
■ Each one is different, but they all have a common theme and a similar format.
■ They are intended for practical use as information tools.

You will also see that databases don't have to contain just words and numbers: they can also contain graphics including diagrams, drawings and photographs.

3.2 Computerized databases

A computer database is simply a file containing records, each arranged in a series of fields.

For instance here is a database record with four fields separated by commas (not commas and spaces, note).

■ 48 Lavender Gardens,Kensington,London,W8 3XG

Many people think that a database has to be created with specialist database management software, such as Microsoft Access, but actually many databases are simple comma-separated or comma-delimited text files. The advantage of this is that such files are easy to create and the file size is fairly small.

Specialist database management software has the additional advantage that you can define the length and format of a field. This reduces file size still further and helps to avoid errors. For instance, you could specify that the post-code field should always be eight characters long (and no more) and that such and such a character could only be a letter (or only a number, or only a space). The database management software would check any new entries and reject them if they weren't the right length or format.

Activity 28

4 mins

Open a simple text editor such as Windows Notepad and type in the following two lines exactly as shown.

Address1,Address2,Address3,Postcode
48 Lavender Gardens,Kensington,London,W8 3XG

Save this file as **flatfile.txt** and close it. (Make sure you save it with the type Text file.)

Now start up Excel and try to open **flatfile.txt**.

What happens? Is Excel able to open the file in a useful form?

There is more information about spreadsheets such as Excel in the workbooks *Solving Problems and Making Decisions* and *Obtaining Information for Effective Management,* in this series.

You should have found that Excel recognized that the file was a sort of database and started up a Wizard to help you import the data in a useful way (in other words with a separate column for each field). Have another go if the Wizard frightened you off and you just clicked on Cancel! Next time follow through the steps and try to get the data into separate columns.

A database may be passive – in other words once compiled it remains unaltered until a new edition is produced. This will be the case with such documents as catalogues and encyclopaedias, and high-tech products such as CD-ROM databases.

However, any database held on a computer can be live and active:

■ 'live' – in the sense that more records may continually be added;
■ 'active' – in the sense that records can be updated as new information comes in.

Here is a typical example of a 'flat file' database, which consists of a single table, in this case one stored in a Microsoft Excel spreadsheet. This shows a standard record, consisting of 18 separate fields (columns A to R), into each of which a particular kind of information can be entered. We've had to split the illustration in two, to fit it on the page: in reality the fields are all in a long row.

	A	B	C	D	E	F	G	H	I
1	Surname	Title	Initials	Account no.	Address1	Address2	Addess3	Town	Postcode
2	Thomas	Mrs	D.W.G	G4577/89	Flat 4	25 Bland Road	Shirley	Birmingham	B29 2AA

	J	K	L	M	N	O	P	Q	R
1	Telephone	Boiler type	Fuel	Year installed	Agreement	Start date	Service month	Last service	Comments
2	0121 621 5878	Hotfyre 2005	Gas	1994	Gold Star Plus	17/03/95	April	14/04/03	Consider replacement boiler early 2004

As you will have realized, this is a record used by a domestic heating system firm (Bajazet Ltd) to record details of customers with whom it has service agreements. There may be many hundreds or even thousands of similar records in its database. (Each row of the spreadsheet is a separate record.)

When Mrs Thomas has a problem with her gas boiler, she phones Bajazet Ltd. A customer service person asks her name and, opening the database on the computer, keys in a search for 'Thomas'. Since this probably comes up with several names, the next step is to ask the customer for some specific identifier. Postcode will probably provide this.

The service person then double-checks with the customer. The record that appears on the computer screen contains information that is relevant to this customer's call, including the type of service agreement and the type of equipment concerned.

Activity 29 · 4 mins

Suggest at least two other practical uses for the information on this record.

_____

_____

_____

The records in this database contain information that the company can use in several ways:

- to administer its revenue – by triggering the issue of invoices and reminders for renewal of the annual service contracts;
- to organize its service operation more efficiently – by planning annual services so as to minimize the distances engineers have to travel;
- to generate sales opportunities – because by knowing the type, age and service history of the customer's installation, it can propose upgrading or replacement;
- to maintain a productive relationship with customers – by writing or telephoning regularly to consult them, reward them for loyalty, make special offers, and so on.

Clearly, such a database has several dimensions. It is a record of personal, technical and operational information. It is also a 'live' record, which is updated whenever necessary, of an important commercial relationship.

3.3 Using databases: mail merge

Firms like Bajazet Ltd often want to write to their customers for various reasons. Under a manual system, they would have two options, neither very attractive:

- send a standard letter (headed 'Dear customer') to everyone;
- process hundreds of letters individually.

With a database, there is a much better option: to generate personalized and addressed letters automatically.

This is done quite simply by creating a document that contains 'slots' for the fields on the database which need to be inserted at that point.

The system will then place the appropriate information from each record selected into the appropriate place in the letter. Large numbers of personalized letters can be generated very quickly in this way.

«Title» «Initials» «Surname»
«Address1»
«Address2»
«Address3»
«Town»
«Postcode»

25 September 2003

Dear «Title» «Surname»

With Winter approaching. we would like to offer you an extra MAINTENANCE CHECK for your «Boiler_type» «Fuel» boiler. This service, which is over and above your normal «Agreement» service, is entirely FREE

Our engineers will be working in the «Town» area on Thursday 18 October. If you would like an engineer to call for your FREE MAINTENANCE CHECK please give us a ring or visit our website and click on 'Winter Offers'.

We would strongly encourage you to take advantage of this offer. Winter is the time when most problems with central heating systems occur. Also. because demand is so high at this time of year, repairs can take longer, and be more expensive.

Please note that engineers will carry out minor repairs and adjustments on the spot for no charge. If more major faults are discovered they may be repaired under the terms of your «Agreement» agreement.

Yours sincerely,

Activity 30

3 mins

Using the data provided in the database example given on page 56 write down the data which is to go into each field (shaded grey in the illustration above) as they would appear after the mail merge. (Don't worry about writing out the whole letter!)

Use a separate sheet of paper for this Activity.

The answer to this question is on pages 107–8.

Similar approaches can be used for generating address labels, and for creating bills, statements and other routine documents.

3.4 Sorting records in a database

In a manual filing system, care has to be taken to put each record in the right place and in the right order, or it can't easily be retrieved. In a computer database, selecting the right place is important – though it's not easy to remove a record accidentally from the database it belongs to. The order, however, is irrelevant.

The computer provides random access retrieval. This means that if you can identify the record or records that you want, the computer will find them wherever they are in the database.

Thus, in our earlier example, the computer first found all the records with the name Thomas in the Surname field, then used the postcode or address fields to whittle these down to the correct one. It doesn't matter when the record was entered into the database or when it was last used.

However, a computer can sort records in various ways. It could sort them by the data in any field, or in combinations of fields such as:

- in alphabetical order of surname and initials, as with a telephone directory;
- by alphabetical order of town, and then by surname;
- by postcode;
- by age of installation;
- by agreement type.

Microsoft Excel can sort a table of data by up to three criteria, for example by column A, then by column C, then by column F. Excel also has an Autofilter facility that you could use, say, to make the database show only records with the surname Thomas, or only records where the surname begins with 'Th'.

The databases you use may well be part of a much larger system such as an accounting system or a customer relationship management system.

If any basic training is available on getting the most out of the system you use there is probably a strong case for getting yourself and some of your team booked up for it.

3.5 Generating reports

Most database programs are able to print out the results of analysis in the form of reports. Given the fairly large amount of data in the Bajazet Ltd database, a large number of reports can be generated.

Once again, reporting uses the database program's ability to select, sort and group records according to the fields and what they contain.

Activity 31

12 mins

Leaving aside the fields in columns A to J which contain customer details, which fields from the Bajazet Ltd database would be used to report on the following matters, and what extra calculations would the system have to do?

1 How many customers are due to have their boilers serviced each month through the year?

_____

_____

2 Which customers have had boilers that are more than 10 years old?

_____

_____

3 Customers ought to receive a sales call offering to quote for replacing the boiler

_____

_____

1 Column P gives the month in which each customer's service is due. The system simply needs to count how many Mays it has, how many Junes and so on.

2 Column M shows the year the boiler was installed. The system needs to count how many records contain a year 'value' that is 10 less than the current year's 'value' (for example 2004 − 10 = 1994).

3 Different boilers have different average lifetimes, so the answer to this question will be found in comparing column K (Boiler type) with column M (Year

installed) and whatever is considered the typical figure for boiler lifetime. The sales team would also have to consider any recommendation for replacement in column R for boilers younger than the normal replacement age.

As you can see, a database like Bajazet's is both powerful and flexible, and you will have noted that the database isn't just about storing data: calculations and logical operations can be done too. So, while commercially available database programs are fairly easy to use at a basic level, to get the most from them requires a fair degree of skill and experience.

Activity 32

10 mins

In your spreadsheet create a column of about 10 to 15 numbers. Create a column next to it where each of the first set of numbers is multiplied by 20.

Sorting and filtering

Suppose you have a list of customers in a spreadsheet like this:

	A	B	C	D	E
1	**Name**	**Title**	**Initial**	**Address**	**Town**
2	Armitage	Mrs	P	4 High St	Bath
3	Bertram	Mr	F	6 Cedar Rd	Newcastle on Tyne
4	Deane	Miss	L	25 Norton Cres	Grimsby
5	Evans	Mr	N	42 Queens Rd	Newcastle on Tyne
6	Fuller	Mr	K	33 Seaview	Torquay
7	Harris	Mrs	O	32 Duke St	Bath
8	Ingrams	Dr	B	78 Long Rd	Maidenhead
9	Jones	Mrs	N	49 Green Rd	Aberystwyth
10	Miles	Mrs	P	3 The Avenue	Edinburgh
11	O'Brien	Miss	R	2 River View	Newcastle on Tyne
12	Pearson	Dr	A	125 Main St	Southsea
13	Smith	Miss	F	50 The Willows	Maidenhead
14	Taylor	Mrs	C	39 South St	Maidenhead
15	Watkins	Mrs	A	19 School Lane	Northampton
16	Young	Mr	A	14 Acacia Av	Preston
17					

The customers are in alphabetical order by last name. You want to target marketing at customers in a particular town. Using the sort function on your spreadsheet, you can display the customer list ordered alphabetically by town.

This groups all the customers in the same town together, like this:

	A	B	C	D	E
	Name	**Title**	**Initial**	**Address**	**Town**
2	Jones	Mrs	N	49 Green Rd	Aberystwyth
3	Armitage	Mrs	P	4 High St	Bath
4	Harris	Mrs	O	32 Duke St	Bath
5	Miles	Mrs	P	3 The Avenue	Edinburgh
6	Deane	Miss	L	25 Norton Cres	Grimsby
7	Ingrams	Dr	B	78 Long Rd	Maidenhead
8	Smith	Miss	F	50 The Willows	Maidenhead
9	Taylor	Mrs	C	39 South St	Maidenhead
10	Bertram	Mr	F	6 Cedar Rd	Newcastle on Tyne
11	Evans	Mr	N	42 Queens Rd	Newcastle on Tyne
12	O'Brien	Miss	R	2 River View	Newcastle on Tyne
13	Watkins	Mrs	A	19 School Lane	Northampton
14	Young	Mr	A	14 Acacia Av	Preston
15	Pearson	Dr	A	125 Main St	Southsea
16	Fuller	Mr	K	33 Seaview	Torquay
17					

If you have a large number of customers and want to display only the customers living in, say, Newcastle on Tyne, you can use the spreadsheet's filter facility to filter out customers living everywhere else. This is the result:

	A	B	C	D	E
1	**Name** ▾	**Tit** ▾	**Initi** ▾	**Address** ▾	**Town** ▾
10	Bertram	Mr	F	6 Cedar Rd	Newcastle on Tyne
11	Evans	Mr	N	42 Queens Rd	Newcastle on Tyne
12	O'Brien	Miss	R	2 River View	Newcastle on Tyne
17					

Graphics

Spreadsheets can also convert data into graphic formats: bar charts, line graphs and pie charts. These can be useful ways of analysing data. You may notice a trend in a graphic that isn't obvious from a set of figures in a table.

4 Spreadsheets

A spreadsheet is not primarily designed for storing information. It *can* be used for storing data, but more often the information will be drawn into it from other sources, such as databases. However, when planning to collect information, think about whether you are going to analyse it using a spreadsheet. This will help you to be clearer about what information you need, how to collect it, and the form in which to store it.

4.1 What is a spreadsheet?

You have probably already come across spreadsheets. At least you may understand that they look like grids in which you type text and numbers. You may have tried to keep track of your personal spending using one.

The grid consists of rows and columns forming a large table, each intersection of a row and column forming a cell, like this one. The cell highlighted in the picture is in column B, row 5 and so is labelled B5 (which you can see in the box above column A). The labelling of cells makes it possible for you to make references to this cell from anywhere else in the spreadsheet by using the cell label instead of having to enter the data again.

For example, if you have entered the annual sales for a product in cell B5 and later want to work out the average monthly sales you can simply enter =B5/12 in another cell anywhere in the worksheet and it will look up the data in cell B5 and divide it by 12. (The equals sign is used to tell the spreadsheet that this is a calculation, and the / sign means 'divide by'.) By the way, you will always need to press 'Enter' after typing in data in a spreadsheet cell, or use one of the arrow keys.

One advantage of storing data in a spreadsheet is the ease with which you can do calculations, from simple addition (+), subtraction (−), division (/) and multiplication (*) to more complex calculations using built-in formulae called functions. There is one function you should know about, and that's the 'Total' function. A set of data (in column C, from row 4 to row 12 in this example) can be totalled by entering the command =SUM(C4:C12) exactly like this, with no spaces. Alternatively you can use the AutoSum facility. This is a short-cut on the toolbar (at the top of the spreadsheet) with the symbol Σ. This is the Greek letter sigma and is used in maths and statistics as shorthand for 'total'. Click on this shortcut and =SUM() will appear in the cell. All you need to do is to drag your mouse down the column or across the row of data you want totalled and it will enter this range (which is what any set of data referred to in any spreadsheet computation is called) into the formula. Press enter and the total appears. (If you chose a cell at the bottom of your column or row of data, the formula will offer this range automatically for you to accept (press enter) unless you choose another set of data.)

Data can be entered in various different formats. For example, the numbers 12345 entered into a cell could be formatted to appear as:

- 12,345 (General)
- 12,345.00 (Number)
- £12,345.00 (Currency)
- 18-Oct-33 (Date)
- 12,34500.00% (Percentage)

The picture shown here is the Format Cells dialogue box in Microsoft® Excel. It appears if you click the right mouse button while a cell is highlighted and select Format Cells. The examples above illustrate some of the options. The Date is based on a sequence which numbers each day from 1st January 1900.

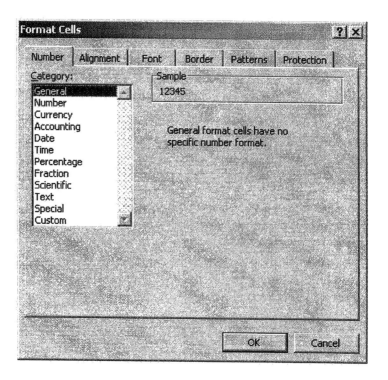

You will need access to spreadsheet software to do the activities in this section. The activities are very basic and it is not possible to give specific instructions, since spreadsheets are all different. You may need to refer to your spreadsheet manual or online Help.

Activity 33

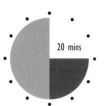

20 mins

Create a spreadsheet that demonstrates that you have the following basic spreadsheet skills. If necessary refer to the user manual or the online Help system for your spreadsheet to find out how to do them. Print out any help pages you use.

■ Enter numbers and format them, for instance make them display as 1,234 (comma format) or 5.67 (to two decimal places) or as a percentage (25% instead of 0.25).
■ Enter dates such as 24/03/2004.
■ Enter text.
■ Select cells, copy and paste their contents and drag them to other parts of the spreadsheet.
■ Sum a column of numbers.

Keep the basic skills spreadsheet file in a safe location on your computer. Note down where it is here.

4.2 Simple uses of spreadsheets

You can store and analyse simple information in a spreadsheet very easily. A good example is keeping records of monthly expenses to claim back from your employer. You could use columns to record the following information:

■ date of expense;
■ description of the expense;
■ total cost;
■ VAT, if your employer needs to know this;
■ separate categories for different types of expense, for example, mileage allowance, hotel costs, car hire, and so on.

Spreadsheets can be used for analysing management information. See the workbook *Obtaining Information for Effective Management* in this series.

At the end of the month, the spreadsheet can total all the columns automatically, and you can transfer the data onto your expenses claim form in whatever way required. Your employer might even accept a printout of a spreadsheet as a claim. Employers usually expect to see receipts and any other paper records of expenses, but for electronic storage, a spreadsheet is probably sufficient.

Inserting data from other programs

You can import data into a spreadsheet from other programs, for example, a word processor or a database. Spreadsheets let you do this in two ways:

- You can usually copy and paste data successfully from almost anywhere.
- If the spreadsheet you are using has a converter for the program where your data is stored, you can import a whole file.

If you are collecting information you want to analyse using a spreadsheet, take a look at how the spreadsheet allows you to import data. This may affect your method of collection. Refer to your spreadsheet's user manual or online Help for information.

Automatic calculations

As you have seen, one of the most useful functions of a spreadsheet is that it can perform calculations on sets of numbers automatically. The most simple is to total up a set of figures. For more complicated calculations you create a formula. The spreadsheet automatically inserts the solution to the formula in the required place.

Activity 34

20 mins

This table shows a set of expenses. Copy the table into a spreadsheet, formatting the cells in the four right-hand columns as being in pounds and pence and calculating the mileage based on 34p per mile, then add the total at the bottom of each column. Highlight the four totals (not the mileage) and use the chart function to create a pie chart of the different types of expense. Use the 'Help' feature of the spreadsheet to guide you.

	Miles	@ 34p	Train	Meals	Other expenses
2nd October	28		£95.00	£5.75	£2.30
11th October	36			£6.00	
13th October	125			£7.99	
18th October	16				£23.01
24th October	227			£4.24	
27th October	28		£95.00		£2.30

Keep the spreadsheet in a safe location on your computer. Note down where it is here:

_____

Spreadsheets and databases are very useful tools. You can use them to store and analyse data for any number of different purposes. It is worth thinking about whether you will be using either of them, and to plan your information collection process accordingly.

Self-assessment 3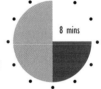

8 mins

1 Define a database.

_____

_____

2 Why are databases particularly useful in marketing?

_____

_____

3 Which of the following could be considered to be a database? Underline your answer/s.

- A library card index catalogue.
- A 'tree' of folders in a computer's file manager.
- A collection of training videos.
- A training manual.

4   Suppose a field in a database is for telephone numbers only, and is 15 characters long.

   ■ Could you accidentally insert a line from an address instead?

   _____

   _____

   ■ What would happen if you tried to insert something 18 characters long?

   _____

   _____

5   List four of the criteria that a database management system will use to sort data.

   _____

   _____

   _____

   _____

6   Enter the table of data below into a spreadsheet and find the answers to the calculations represented by these spreadsheet functions:

   ■ =SUM(A1:A4)   _____

   ■ =A1*B1   _____

   ■ =A2/D2   _____

   ■ =E1*20   _____

   ■ =(A2+A3)/E1   _____

	A	B	C	D	E	F
1	12	£2.00			.5	
2	16			4		
3	10					
4	4					

Answers to these questions can be found on page 104.

5 Summary

- A database is a collection of records arranged to allow quick and easy identification of specific information.

- Databases make it possible to both store and use data more efficiently.

- They are particularly useful for analysing activities such as sales, and for marketing purposes.

- Databases are often used by customer service representatives so as to have all of a customer's details at their fingertips when they are dealing with an enquiry.

- Databases can also be used to manipulate the data they extract (for example perform calculations with it) to generate a wide variety of reports to help manage the business.

Session D
Access control, security and data protection

1 Introduction

Everyone who uses a computer for storing, processing and retrieving information has had their share of unpleasant experiences. Not many computer users receive formal training, and we tend to depend on trial and error.

Most errors aren't important: but losing data can be a catastrophe, and it happens all too often.

1.1 Example: catastrophe!

Davina was under heavy pressure to complete a new procedural manual by Monday morning. She toiled away at the keyboard all weekend, and long into Sunday night, keeping a backup copy of the file on a floppy disk for safety. At about 4 a.m. on Monday morning she was at last happy with the result, but very tired. Before printing out the final version, she decided to back up the file for the last time. Disaster! In her tired state she copied from Drive A (the floppy) to Drive C (the hard disk), instead of the other way round. As a result an older version of the file was over-written on drive C and the final version was lost. Everything she'd done since 7.30 p.m. the previous night was wasted. There was nothing for it but to do it all again.

Perhaps no one really takes data backup seriously until something like this happens. And then it is often possible to recover lost data without too much difficulty. Nevertheless, such problems have a nasty habit of occurring at the last moment, as in Davina's case. So you have been warned!

In this session we will also review ways of securing IT equipment and data against both interference and theft.

Finally we'll explain your responsibilities for protecting other people's data under current UK legislation.

2 Managing risks

Because you can't see or touch a computer file – because it consists of tiny bits of electricity and dots of light on a screen – electronic data can feel very 'slippery' and easy to lose or damage.

Actually, electronic information is pretty tough stuff, though it does need looking after. However, so do traditional stores of information. Paper-based records can be affected by fire, damp, fungus, and by insects that eat away at them. Chemicals in the paper and the effect of light destroy paper and ink.

Even film isn't permanent: many early films and photographic negatives are now decaying.

Of course these are long-term processes. Perhaps more important is simply losing track of important items, as we explained in Session A.

2.1 Protecting electronic information

Any information that you store on a computer is at risk. If there is just one copy, and if that is destroyed, the information may be lost forever. An electronic file is at risk from several directions.

■ **Risks to the hardware**
The computer itself may be damaged or even destroyed. Here are some of the risks:

- fire, and the effects of fire-fighting;
- insects or mice chewing cables (yes, it has happened more than once);

- dust or smoke;
- liquid, ranging from a very humid atmosphere, to a spillage of tea, to a flood;
- excessive heat;
- strong magnetic fields;
- electrical power surges;
- being dropped, and other physical shocks.

Finally, there is the simple risk of breakdown. If a component fails, it may be difficult or even impossible to retrieve the data stored inside the computer.

Activity 35

People are often careless with their computers. Suggest a few simple rules that you could apply at work to protect computer hardware from damage.

_____

_____

_____

_____

_____

The over-riding rule is don't do anything that you wouldn't do to your TV at home. We could add some more rules.

- Don't place drinks or other liquids on or near the computer.
- Don't place the computer where it can easily be knocked or kicked, or where it is subject to strong vibrations or electro-magnetic fields.
- Don't move the computer around more than strictly necessary.
- If you have to move the machine – even to insert or remove a plug at the back – save and close all current files and switch the machine off first.

Other precautions could include using power surge protectors.

- **Risks to the disks**

There is a particular category of hardware risk. A computer's hard disk is read by moveable 'heads', which are located extremely close to the disk as it spins at high speeds. If one of the heads or some other component should touch the disk surface it will plough up vast amounts of data in milliseconds.

Severe physical damage to a hard disk is every computer user's nightmare. Fortunately most hard disks these days are sealed units so they are hard to damage accidentally.

Floppy disks are also vulnerable to damage by bits of dust or grit, heat or liquid. Floppy disks are magnetic media, and strong magnetic fields can destroy or distort the data stored on them. This doesn't often happen, but cases have been known of disks being damaged by being stood on top of powerful loud-speakers (speakers contain large magnets).

Optical disks (CDs and DVDs) are more difficult to damage than floppy disks, but don't make the mistake of thinking they are indestructible. They are sensitive to heat, fingerprints and scratching.

■ **Software and hardware errors**

Computers can go wrong and can make mistakes, though this is not common. When they do go wrong, data can be lost and files can be jumbled up.

■ **Risks of power failure**

Apart from portable notebook computers, which have several hours running time on battery power, computers are dependent on the electricity supply.

2.2 An example of risks

A small company processed most of its work through four computers. One day there was a sudden power cut which was restored again within half a minute. One of the computers was not switched on at the time and was not affected. Of the other three, two were not permanently affected, though a certain amount of current work was lost. One machine, however, developed a serious fault. The maintenance company said that the motherboard (which contains the computer's main logic components) would have to be replaced at a cost of several hundred pounds.

The company claimed and won compensation against the local water company, whose employees had damaged electricity cables while digging a trench nearby.

2.3 Recovery

When data items are 'lost', the loss is seldom complete, unless the storage medium – the disk itself – is either badly damaged or destroyed altogether. Because files are recorded magnetically or optically on the disk, the contents can often be recovered even when they seem to have disappeared completely.

This is possible because of the way the computer's filing system works.

When you save a file, the system first looks for space on the disk. A large file may be broken up into several smaller chunks to fit various gaps on the disk. The system then identifies the electronic address of each storage location, and tags it so that it is listed in the file directory. Finally, it stores the data.

When you retrieve the file, the system searches for the right addresses, and reads the data stored there.

When you delete a file, the system does not delete the data, only the address. The data remains, but is now invisible to the file manager system. The next lot of data you save may be stored on top of the original data, but until this happens, the original material can be recovered using special utility programs.

In practice, it is surprisingly difficult to destroy the data on a disk. Experts can often recover items of data even after determined efforts have been made to eliminate them. The process can be slow and expensive, but when the need is great enough (for instance in a criminal case), it may be done.

The persistence of magnetically stored data can present a security problem. Only physical destruction or repeated overwriting or reformatting of the whole disk can remove all traces of data files. Organizations that are security sensitive may prefer to destroy rather than resell obsolete machines for this reason.

For most computer users, lost files and corrupt data present a serious problem, even if recovery is technically possible because:

- important files can be unavailable for lengthy periods;
- hours or even days of work may have to be redone;
- hours may have to be spent combing through files to see how much loss or damage there is;
- recovery, if done by specialists, may be expensive.

2.4 Backup

The obvious way to protect electronic data is to make another copy, and store it somewhere else. This is called backup: it ensures that if the worst comes to the worst, the effects of losing data are minimized.

Since it is easy to make copies, computer users only have themselves to blame if they don't make backups.

Backups can be done in several ways.

Some programs automatically retain the most recent version of a file (perhaps with the extension .bak) so that you can return to it if you make a mess of the current version.

Others can be set to make backups of all current files every few minutes, minimizing the amount of work lost if the program crashes or there is a power cut.

It is obviously safer to make backups on separate disks or other media rather than on the machine's internal hard disk.

Here are some routine backup procedures.

- Copying current files onto floppy disks or CD-Rs, which are then removed and stored elsewhere.
- Backing up selected folders from each computer on a network onto the hard disk of a server computer.
- Copying the whole contents of a hard disk onto a tape backup device (tape streamer).

Activity 36 · 40 mins

Many organizations do not have thorough, consistent and mandatory backup systems for their data, and sooner or later this is bound to lead to trouble.

Check your organization's general policy on data backup, if there is one, and note down the main points.

Consider how well this policy is applied in your own department, section, etc. Then compare what happens in at least one other section.

What improvements would you recommend? If this includes acquiring new equipment, what would this be?

Draw up a simple set of rules for backup in your own department, and do what you can to ensure that it is implemented.

If your organization is particularly dependent on its computers, it may have gone much further than simple backup measures. It may have opted to back up its whole operation at a different site, perhaps with the assistance of a specialized services company. You'll be glad to know that large organizations such as banks and building societies have arrangements like this.

2.5 Precautions against theft

Computers and peripheral devices are expensive, and are attractive to thieves and burglars. Even small items like disks and computer cables are valuable. General precautions against theft should apply, but there are some specific things that can be done to protect computer equipment.

- They can be 'plated', i.e. bolted to the working surface, or 'caged' in a burglar-proof metal case.
- They can be fitted with alarms.
- They can be security tagged. This doesn't prevent them being stolen, but may deter a thief because it increases the risk of them – and the thief – subsequently being traced.
- Theft of fairly minor items of hardware, such as disks and cables, may seem unimportant, but bear these points in mind.
- The disks have a money value, and they may also contain data files that would be difficult or impossible to replace.
- While cables, etc. can easily be replaced, they too have a money value, and until they are replaced the computer or network may be unusable.

Activity 37

4 mins

Thieves and burglars are usually in a hurry, and computers are generally fairly bulky objects that are tied together by a tangle of wires and cables. Thieves are therefore likely to prefer smaller objects that are easy to remove, carry and conceal.

Look around your working area, and list some of the computer-related items that may be at risk, especially any items that are left out for long periods, including overnight.

_____

_____

_____

_____

_____

Some organizations take considerable care to reduce risks of casual theft by locking away all such items, but this often isn't the case.

Losing disks with information on them is potentially the biggest danger. This is an even bigger risk with the growth of computer component theft. This is when burglars with some computer knowledge open up the computer boxes and remove the most valuable components, such as the central processing chip, the memory chips, the hard disk and expansion cards. Without these, the machine is crippled, and the thieves can make an easy getaway.

2.6 Insurance

It's vital for organizations to insure their IT equipment fully.

■ Hardware and software should be insured at replacement cost.
■ Care should be taken to include all the small items that we discussed above, since their total value can be surprisingly high.
■ Loss of files, information and data should also be insured against.

It may appear difficult to put a value on a file held on a hard disk, but it is realistic to think about matters such as:

■ the working hours put into creating it;
■ the consequences of not having it available.

The loss of a file such as a customer database, possibly together with the backup disks, could be extremely damaging. Such potential losses can be covered by consequential loss insurance. Insurers will typically impose conditions, such as strengthened security and rigorous procedures for backing up data and protecting equipment when not in use. You should ensure that you and your team comply with any requirements.

2.7 Precautions against viruses

Computer viruses cast a curious light on human nature. They are not natural phenomena, like the flu or hepatitis viruses. They have been deliberately created by malicious people in order to cause damage to other people's interests. Unfortunately, there are many thousands in existence, and they can be 'caught' very easily. Software viruses are usually designed to hide away or disguise themselves as something else. These days they are usually transmitted through communications links such as email, but removable disks can also be carriers of viruses.

Activity 38

What action would you take if you saw this appear on your computer screen?

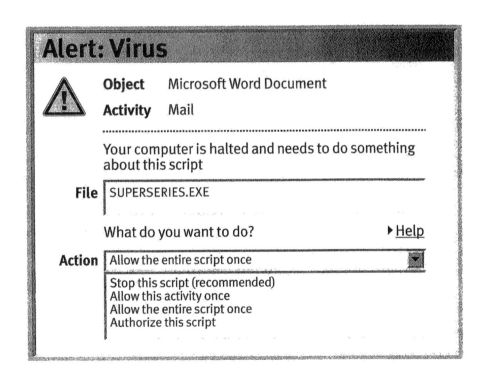

Clearly the recommended action to 'stop this script' is the best choice here.

If a virus enters a large system or a network the damage can be enormous. Files, data and system software can all be attacked. Most organizations therefore respond by:

- using virus protection software, which seeks out and destroys suspicious items;
- banning staff from introducing any disks that haven't been virus-checked by the IT department;
- ensuring that any new software entering the organization is checked before it is released for use.

You can help yourself simply by being careful: never open an email attachment unless you trust the person who sent it and you are absolutely sure you know what the attachment is.

Of course the people who create viruses are always working on new and more deadly ones, so there is a constant race between attackers and defenders. All computer users should check for updates to their anti-virus software very frequently – at least once a week. Many companies have so-called 'Firewalls', which are sophisticated systems to block viruses.

2.8 Emails and security

Viruses are transmitted most often by emails, and any organization or individual with any sense has an up-to-date security system to ensure that their system is as secure as possible against viruses sent this way. However, there are other dangers in emails that you need to be aware of. The most ubiquitous are spam emails, mass mailings of emails that target hundreds of thousands or millions of people with everything from low cost pharmaceuticals to '419 Fraud'. This latter is named after a particular code in Nigerian criminal law, and involves targets being asked to help move large sums of money from hidden bank accounts, often in Nigeria (hence the Nigerian connection) but it could be from anywhere. Unfortunately there is the need for some cash to enable the transfer to be made, and victims are asked to pay over several thousand pounds in advance fees, in return for a share of the millions involved.

How do these scams work and why are they worth doing? Because the cost of sending an email is effectively nil, once the Internet connection is paid for, the only cost is to obtain email addresses. This can be done in a number of ways, including using software agents that search websites for email addresses or create a series of 'name@' to put in front of legitimate web addresses (e.g. susan@superseries.com, david@superseries.co, etc.). Why do it? If the spammers get a 0.1% response rate from 10 m emails, and each person pays £25 for goods, then that's £250,000 income!

As well as anti-virus you can also have anti-spam security software, which helps reduce the scale of the problem, as email inboxes can easily get clogged up with these menaces. If you receive an email from someone you don't know and who has no legitimate right to know your email address, do not respond, as this provides proof of your address. Instead you can add them to your 'Blocked senders' list, to stop them getting through again. If they offer an 'unsubscribe' option you could use this, but this can be the way that some spammers confirm your address.

Unfortunately too many of your fellow employees are also spammers, although they would not realize their guilt. Forwarding emails with jokes, gossip and links to amusing websites wastes time and uses up bandwidth (the capacity of the organization's IT system). So does using the 'Reply to all' button, when only one person needs to know. If someone forwards irrelevant material or 'Replies to all' unnecessarily, point this out to them (politely). If it continues, you could add them to your 'Blocked senders' list as well.

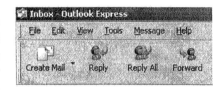

Under the Privacy and Electronic Communications (EC Directive) Regulations 2003, unsolicited electronic communications (email and SMS text messages) can only be sent to people who have opted in to receive them, and they must show clearly who has sent them. These regulations also make unsolicited fax marketing illegal, and give legal force to the telephone and mail preference services (to stop unsolicited telephone sales and junk mail). However, most spammers originate outside the EU and so evade the law, unfortunately.

3 Data security

Information held on computers or in filing cabinets or desk storage needs to be protected from interference and prying eyes. Interference may be just casual – someone playing around with your computer or the files on your desk when you're not there – but it can still result in damage, disruption or loss of files. In the case of paper records, security will involve locks on filing cabinets and desk drawers that contain sensitive information of any kind; keys need to be kept by a minimum number of authorized personnel and files should never be left lying about. There should be a proper system for recording when files are removed, and by whom, and for ensuring that they are returned. A 'clear desk' policy means that all work materials are removed from the desk surface and locked away before the person working at each desk leaves the office.

Security involves both the prevention of information passing into the wrong hands (your organization's competitors, for instance) and the prevention of alteration of data. Such alterations may not be immediately noticeable.

3.1 Example: data alteration

If unauthorized people can access files, for example if there is no password protection on computers, it is possible that files may be altered without the knowledge of those who use the files. Financial records and disciplinary records are examples of the sort of material that unauthorized personnel might have dishonest reasons for wishing to change. Changes leave a trace in the system, because the computer will always record when a file was last changed. Nonetheless, if you do not know with certainty when the last authorized change was made, it may not be apparent that subsequent changes were mischievous. Even if you know the date of the last authorized change, would you remember to check every time you access a file, that it has not been tampered with since? Would you be able to detect exactly what had been changed? It is better to prevent unauthorized access in the first place, than to try to detect it after it has happened!

3.2 Preventing unauthorized access

Activity 39

4 mins

Think about the data and information held on your own computer. What files would you prefer your line manager/team/other colleagues not to have access to?

How can you prevent them from doing so?

_____

_____

_____

Most computers have a rather flimsy little lock on the front, but this would not deter a determined 'hacker'. It is also possible to buy locks for floppy disk slots, making it difficult for someone to copy files. However, few users seem to bother with such precautions.

Switching off the machine when it is not attended is often recommended. This would prevent casual snoopers from reading files on the screen. Unfortunately, this won't always be possible or desirable, especially when the user moves around a lot and the machine is needed continuously.

Some users disguise their most sensitive files by giving them uninformative file names or placing them in unexpected parts of the directory.

Some programs allow users to attach passwords to particular files. The file cannot then be opened unless the correct password is keyed in.

A useful approach is to attach a password to a screen saver. The original screen can only be restored by keying in the password.

Activity 40

4 mins

Think about the two strategies we have just mentioned: disguising files and using passwords. What drawbacks occur to you?

_____

_____

_____

_____

Passwords can be a problem because:

- many people use a password that is fairly obvious, such as their nickname, or the name of a partner or child;
- others choose a less obvious password and then forget it altogether;

- many people write down their password where someone might find it;
- hiding files away carries similar risks: the user may not be able to find them either!

Passwords are useful as a protection against non-expert snoopers and against accidental alterations, though they may not prevent a file from being deleted. Experts are unlikely to be baffled for long by the basic password systems that most popular programs use: for instance you can freely download software from the Internet that enables you to 'crack' the passwords used by Microsoft Office programs with ease.

3.3 More sophisticated systems

Large-scale and networked computer systems are likely to be protected from unauthorized use in more sophisticated ways. These include:

- extensive use of passwords and regular changing of all passwords;
- centrally controlled restrictions to limit the levels and range of access available to particular terminals;
- auditing or tracking software that can register what terminals or passwords were used to access particular files, and when.

In big systems it's particularly important to prevent files from being deleted or amended without authorization. The operating programs may be designed to prevent this happening. For example, many users may need to access a database file in order to retrieve information, but only one computer may be allowed to make changes or additions to the database.

In a slightly different context, where several people are working on a project at the same time, some system of authorization, control, backup and reporting will be needed. The aim is to ensure that everyone is working on the right version, and that they don't make contradictory changes to the file. This is relevant in a variety of situations, including:

- project management;
- architectural design;
- other product and system design;
- authoring of major publications;
- multimedia design;
- software design and development.

4 The law and data storage

Data protection legislation is the response to public concern about organizations that collect, store and use information about people.

Activity 41

4 mins

Why do you think people might object to organizations keeping information about them?

_____

_____

Many people feel unhappy about their personal details being retained by commercial organizations. Here are some of the concerns that people have.

- Incorrect details may be entered, causing anything from minor irritation to significant financial problems.
- A list or database may be sold to other organizations, who then try to sell various goods and services to the people on it.
- 'Personalized' mailings may arrive addressed to someone who has recently died, causing great distress to the surviving partner.

4.1 Example: the need for data protection

Lynn applied for a small bank loan, only to be refused. Soon after, her credit card company wrote cancelling the card and demanding settlement of the account. Lynn was astounded, and at first could get no explanation.

Eventually it turned out that the problem was data held by a credit reference agency. Lynn lived in a small village called Oxleigh, and her postal address was 25 High Street, Oxleigh, followed by the name of the nearby town. Someone who lived at 25 High Street **in the nearby town** had defaulted on a loan and a County Court judgement had been made against them.

The credit reference agency was unable to distinguish between the two addresses, and hence Lynn was unable to get credit of any kind. It took three years for this mess to be sorted out.

4.2 The Data Protection Act 1998

EXTENSION 4
Further information and guidance about the *Data Protection Act* is available from the website.

Data protection legislation was introduced in the early 1980s to try to prevent some of these abuses. The latest version is the Data Protection Act 1998.

The Act is concerned with 'personal data', which is information about living, identifiable individuals. This can be as little as a name and address: it need not be particularly sensitive information. If it is sensitive, which is explained further on in this section, then extra care is needed.

The Act gives individuals (data subjects) certain rights, and it requires those who record and use personal information (data controllers) to be open about their use of that information and to follow 'sound and proper practices' (the data protection principles).

4.3 The eight data protection principles

Data must be:

- fairly and lawfully processed;
- processed for limited purposes;
- adequate, relevant and not excessive;
- accurate;
- not kept longer than necessary;
- processed in accordance with individuals' rights;
- secure;
- not transferred to countries that do not have adequate data protection laws.

If your organization holds personal information about living individuals on computer or has such information processed on computer by others (for example, its accountants or auditors) your organization probably needs to 'notify' under the Data Protection Act 1998.

'Notify' means that the organization has to complete a form about the data it holds and how it is used and send it, with an annual registration fee, to the office of the Information Commissioner.

The Data Protection Act 1998 also covers some records held in paper form. These do not need to be notified to the Commissioner, but they should also be handled in accordance with the data protection principles. A set of index cards for a personnel system is a typical example of paper records that fall under the Data Protection Act 1998.

4.4 Fair processing for limited purposes

These two principles mean that when an organization collects information from individuals it should be honest and open about why it wants the information and it should have a legitimate reason for processing the data. For instance, organizations should explain who they are, what they intend to use the information for and who, if anybody, they intend to give the personal data to.

4.5 Adequate, relevant and not excessive; accurate and no longer than necessary

Organizations should hold neither too much nor too little data about the individuals in their list. For instance, many companies collect date of birth or age range information from their customers, but in many cases all they actually need to know is that they are over eighteen.

Personal data should be accurate and up-to-date as far as possible. However, if individuals provide inaccurate information (for example lie about their age) the organization would not normally be held to account for this.

There are only exceptional circumstances where personal data should be kept indefinitely. Data should be removed when it is no longer required for audit purposes or when a customer ceases to do business with you.

4.6 The rights of data subjects

Individuals have various rights including:

■ the right to be informed of all the information held about them by an organization;
■ the right to prevent the processing of their data for the purposes of direct marketing;

■ the right to compensation if they can show that they have been caused damage by any contravention of the Act;

■ the right to have any inaccurate data about them removed or corrected.

Organizations have obligations if they receive a written request from individuals asking to see what data it holds about them, or to obtain a copy of it, or to be given an explanation of what it is used for, or who it is given to. The organization must deal with the request promptly, and in any case within 40 days. The organization is entitled, if it wishes, to ask for a fee of not more than £10, in which case the 40 days does not begin until this is received.

Activity 42

It is important that your staff know how to recognize a subject access request and realize that it must be dealt with urgently. Customers may not mention the Data Protection Act 1998 at all – they may just say: 'Could you tell me what info you've got about me?'

Draw up a policy for your team members, explaining briefly what they should do if they receive such a request, including what they should do if the request is part of a telephone conversation.

4.7 Security

Organizations should make sure that they provide adequate security for the data, taking into account the nature of the data, and the possible harm to the individual that could arise if the data is disclosed or lost. This means security measures such as we discussed earlier in this session, including the following.

■ Measures to ensure that access to computer records by staff is authorized (for instance a system of passwords).

■ Measures to control access to records by people other than staff. For instance care should be taken over the siting of computers to prevent casual callers to the organization's premises being able to read personal data on screen. Also there should be procedures to verify the identity of callers (especially telephone callers) seeking information about an individual.

■ Measures to prevent the accidental loss or theft of personal data, for example backups and fire precautions.

4.8 Overseas transfers

If an organization wishes to transfer personal data to a country outside the European Economic Area (EEA) it will either need to ensure there is adequate protection (for example a Data Protection Act) for the data in the receiving country, or obtain the consent of the individual.

All countries in the EEA already have suitable protection.

4.9 Sensitive data

The Act defines eight categories of sensitive personal data. If an organization holds personal data falling into these categories it is likely that it will need the explicit consent of the individual concerned. It will also need to ensure that its security is adequate for the protection of sensitive data.

Here are the eight categories:

■ The racial or ethnic origin of data subjects.
■ Their political opinions.
■ Their religious beliefs or other beliefs of a similar nature.
■ Whether they are members of a trade union.
■ Their physical or mental health or condition.
■ Their sexual life.
■ The commission or alleged commission by them of any offence.
■ Any details of court proceedings or sentences against them.

4.10 Enforcement

If an organization is breaching the principles of the Act, the Commissioner has various powers to force it to comply, including issuing an enforcement notice, and the power to enter and search their premises, and examine equipment and documents. It is an offence to obstruct the Commissioner, and there are also fines and criminal penalties for holding data without being registered, for failing to comply with an enforcement notice, and for unauthorized disclosure of personal data.

Activity 43

4 mins

Does your department need to access databases that are registered under the Act? If so, try to find out what they are (the legal department or company secretary's office will know) and list them here.

_____

_____

_____

_____

Personal data may be kept for any of several dozen different reasons, although the data of main interest under the Act are kept for sales, marketing and promotional purposes. If you believe that you or your department are holding data that should be registered, or you are unsure what can be disclosed to whom, you should discuss the matter with your line manager.

Self-assessment 4 ·

10 mins

1   It is unwise to leave a floppy disk containing data on a sunny windowsill. Why?

_____

2   List five risks to computer hardware.

_____

_____

_____

_____

3   When you tell a computer to delete a file, what actually happens, and why may it be possible to recover the file?

_____

_____

4 How could you reduce the risk of viruses entering your organization's computers?

_____

_____

5 What are the eight data protection principles?

_____

_____

_____

_____

_____

_____

_____

_____

6 You believe that Cosmic & Universal Credit Providers Ltd may hold incorrect information about you in its computer files. What are your main rights under the Data Protection Act 1998?

_____

_____

7 Give three examples of 'sensitive data' under the Data Protection Act 1998.

_____

_____

_____

Answers to these questions can be found on pages 105–6.

5 Summary

- Both equipment and data need protecting from risks such as physical damage, theft, unauthorized interference and viruses.

- Computers and storage media are fairly sturdy, but they can be damaged. The risks include:
  - heat, dust and smoke;
  - liquids and damp;
  - strong magnetic fields and power surges;
  - physical shocks.

- Loss of data can sometimes be a serious problem. However, data that is accidentally deleted from a disk can often be recovered, providing the user acts quickly.

- Taking backups is the first line of defence: all computer users should ensure that they take backup copies at regular intervals.

- Equipment, including easy-to-steal accessories, disks, etc. should be properly secured and fully insured.

- Computer viruses can be a serious problem. The best solution is to keep anti-virus software running constantly on your computer and make sure that it is updated at least weekly.

- Unauthorized access to computers and data can be prevented with security hardware, passwords and simple precautions like switching the machine off when not in use.

- The Data Protection Act 1998 is concerned with information about living, identifiable individuals. The Act gives individuals certain rights and it requires organizations that record and use personal information to follow the eight data protection principles.

Performance checks

1 Quick quiz

Write down your answers in the spaces below to the following questions on *Understanding Workplace Information Systems*.

Question 1   How long should an organization keep its banking records and why?

_____

_____

Question 2   How long should you keep an email from your manager about the work schedule for next week, and why?

_____

_____

Question 3   Many organizations digitally photograph their older paper records and store the images on media such as CD-ROM.

True/False

Question 4   What computer storage medium offers the largest capacity?

_____

_____

Question 5   A letter from a business named Jason King Consultants Ltd would most probably be filed as:

     a   Consultants, Jason King Ltd
     b   Jason King Consultants Ltd
     c   King (Jason), Consultants Ltd

Question 6   When does it become useful to use a system of cross-referencing? And in what circumstances is an index useful?

_____

_____

Question 7   One of the following is not a valid computer file name. Which one, and why?

     a   0015550.001
     b   b-target.5tg
     c   A> Z.doc
     d   daisy2

_____

_____

Question 8   It is usually quicker to do a computer search for a file using part of the name than to search for files containing specific text.

True or False?

Question 9   In a database table:

The records are laid out as _____.

The fields are laid out as _____.

Enter 'rows' or 'columns' as appropriate.

Question 10   What are the advantages of mail merge?

_____

_____

Question 11   Why is it sometimes not suitable to use a spreadsheet as a database?

_____

_____

_____

Question 12 Files accidentally deleted from a disk can often be recovered provided that … what?

Question 13 What is the best way to avoid losing a computer file?

Question 14 Which of these is the most secure password, and why?

a sgp
b letmein
c c3M260tpX53
d susanj

Question 15 If you take a laptop computer containing personal data about customers to the USA you are breaking the Data Protection Act 1998.

True or False?

Answers to these questions can be found on pages 108–9.

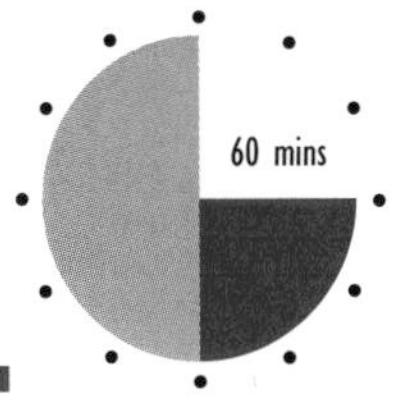

2 Workbook assessment

Read the following case incident and then deal with the questions that follow, writing your answers on a separate sheet of paper.

Vincent is in charge of building repairs and maintenance at a large college campus. His four-strong team is responsible for:

- urgent repairs: replacing broken locks and fixing leaking roofs, etc.;
- planned maintenance: painting, decorating, weather-proofing and checking and repairing defects in the structure.

The maintenance unit works to an annual budget set by the Site Administrator to whom Vincent reports. The budget covers wage costs, overtime, training, materials and equipment. There is also a small budget for sub-contractors.

Vincent's administrative system is entirely paper-based. He types his reports manually, and writes out job sheets and dockets by hand.

Because the administration is trying to cut costs, the maintenance team's activities and budgets are to be scrutinized more carefully. Vincent will in future have to:

- reduce stocks of materials and equipment;
- purchase materials more competitively;
- seek formal approval for all jobs, including urgent repairs;
- submit cost estimates, that is report on – and justify – the actual cost of each job.

To make this easier; the college will supply Vincent with a computer system and appropriate software and training.

- **What documentation will be required under the new system?**
- **What records will Vincent need to keep?**
- **What computer hardware and software will be appropriate?**
- **What training would you recommend?**

Reflect and review

1 Reflect and review

Now that you have completed your work on *Understanding Workplace Information Systems*, let us review the objectives that we set at the beginning.

Our first objective was to:

■ **explain the principles behind any system for storing and retrieving information and the key content that organizations are likely to record.**

These days we tend to think in terms of digital technology for information storage, but manual systems are still relevant and widely used. The traditional filing cabinet has not yet had its day!

The basic principles of information storage will always be as follows.

- What is stored must also be readily retrievable.
- Storage must therefore be organized in a systematic way.
- The information must be protected from damage, deterioration and interference.
- The storage and retrieval systems must be as convenient and economical as possible.
- You should be applying these four rules to any information storage that you undertake. If there is any aspect that is not quite up to standard, what would you propose to do about it?

_____

_____

As to what information should be kept, this is partly determined by legal requirements and partly by organizational needs to do with operational efficiency, finance and decision making.

■ Are you clear about your organization's document retention policy? Is it properly applied in your department? Perhaps you keep too much.

_____

_____

The technology of data storage is developing extremely quickly. New methods and new media are entering the marketplace, and storage capacities are soaring. At the same time, the basic index of cost – pence per Megabyte – is falling.

It will be important for you to keep abreast of the technology, which explains our second objective.

■ **describe and evaluate the range of data storage media presently available.**

Evaluating means considering the costs, the benefits and the possible risks and disadvantages of the new media as they come along. Bearing in mind that new kinds of drive are often needed to play the media, this is not always a simple matter. Certainly it will mean regularly reading one or more of the major computer monthlies.

■ Make a list of the storage media that you are least familiar with, and note briefly how you propose to extend your knowledge.

_____

_____

Although most storage media – including the latest ones – are random-access (i.e. files don't have to be stored in any particular order), in practice it is important to be systematic about data storage.

This is particularly true when the number of files stored grows large. The computer won't lose them, but the user might forget the filenames, folders or disks under which they are stored.

Hence our next objective is to:

■ **organize the systematic and secure storage of data in manual and computer-based systems.**

This applies to both the general way you arrange your working files, and so on, and also to the measures you take to look after them. If you have not already done so, you might consider reviewing and reorganizing the way your manual and computer files are organized.

Are there any particular matters that have come to your attention as a result of reading this book, for example a large number of documents filed under 'miscellaneous' or still awaiting filing?

Has valuable data or equipment ever been damaged or lost in your department?

- Make a note of what you intend to do to avoid these problems in the future.

_____

_____

Our next objective was to:

- **identify the use and application of databases and spreadsheets.**

It's quite possible that you already use a database or spreadsheet in your day-to-day work, although you may only use a database via a user-friendly front-end program, such as an accounting package or a marketing system.

- Is there a case for receiving extra training in the use of your organization's databases, or for having 'stand-alone' database software such as Microsoft Access on your computer? If so write down the arguments here, so that you can persuade your line manager that it will make you more effective in your job.

_____

_____

- Would you benefit from more advanced testing in using spreadsheets to analyse data? If so, write down some of the uses you think you could make of this extra knowledge & skill to improve your performance as a manager.

_____

_____

Our final objective was to:

- **outline the law on data protection.**

The Data Protection Act 1998 is concerned with information about living, identifiable individuals and it includes certain paper records, not just computerized information. The Act gives individuals certain rights and it requires organizations that record and use personal information to follow the eight data protection principles.

■ Read through the eight principles listed in Session D. Can you confidently say that you and your colleagues are abiding by these principles? Comment briefly on any problems that you think might arise.

_____

_____

2 Action plan

Use this plan to further develop for yourself a course of action you want to take. Make a note in the left-hand column of the issues or problems you want to tackle, and then decide what you intend to do, and make a note in column 2.

The resources you need might include time, materials, information or money. You may need to negotiate for some of them, but they could be something easily acquired, like half an hour of somebody's time, or a chapter of a book. Put whatever you need in column 3. No plan means anything without a time-scale, so put a realistic target completion date in column 4.

Finally, describe the outcome you want to achieve as a result of this plan, whether it is for your own benefit or advancement, or a more efficient way of doing things.

Desired outcomes				
1 Issues	2 Action	3 Resources	4 Target completion
Actual outcomes				

3 Extensions

Extension 1

Book   *Taming the Paper Tiger at Work*
Author   Barbara Hemphill
Edition   2002
Publisher   Kiplinger Books
ISBN   0938721984

A guide to organizing your office and managing paperwork so that you may become more productive and experience less stress.

Extension 2

Storage media – the latest developments

Major monthly computer magazines such as PC World, MacUser and so on. Study both articles and advertisements to keep track of falling prices and the ever-growing range of options.

Extension 3

Book   *Quick Course in Microsoft Access 2002* (or look for earlier editions for older versions; later editions for more recent versions)
Author   Not named
Edition   2002
Publisher   Online Training Solutions, Inc (formerly Microsoft Press International)
ISBN   1582780706

Extension 4

Data Protection Act 1998

Extensive information and guidance (including a link to the full text of the Act, how to register and so on) are available at the website of the office of the Information Commissioner.

http://www.ico.gov.uk/

4 Answers to self-assessment questions

Self-assessment 1 on pages 21–2

1   The most important reason is because it is a legal requirement to keep many sorts of records.

2   You could have chosen any three from the following list: logs or diaries, job sheets, labour and materials cost records, stock records, plans, budgets, multi-part forms, double-entry records, post records.

3   Paper-based systems are still common because organizations still receive a lot of paper, even if their own systems are entirely computerized, because many organizations like to have written evidence of certain matters, and because older records may occasionally be useful, even though it is not worth converting them to a computerized form.

4   In any large filing system, the document will probably be lost forever.

5   ■ Electronic storage media have great and rapidly growing storage capacity.
    ■ They are very compact compared with other methods.
    ■ The process of storing data is quick and easy.
    ■ Many storage media allow data to be retrieved equally quickly and easily.

6   These are the most likely storage media:

    ■ for a multimedia encyclopaedia: a CD-ROM;
    ■ for data backup: a file server's hard disk or a tape streamer;
    ■ for operating systems and frequently used applications: individual computers' hard disks.

Self-assessment 2 on pages 45–6

I   Being systematic about the storage of information means the following.

    ■ Having safe places **TO STORE IT**.
    ■ Sorting and organizing the information **INTO MEANINGFUL CATEGORIES**.
    ■ Putting it into the right places **PROMPTLY** and **REGULARLY**.
    ■ Being consistent about its **FORMAT AND CONTENT**.

2   Name   Department
    Subject matter   Product
    Date   Customer type
    Geography

3   1st Class Cleaners Ltd
    AAA Builders Ltd
    Burr Martin & Co, Messrs
    Customs and Excise, HM
    Electricity, London
    Firth, Dr G
    Harrish
    Harris-Lane
    London, Jack
    Macey, Roger
    McLean, Albert
    Maclean, Anna

4 Subject organization often leads to overlaps or large numbers of documents filed under a miscellaneous heading. Geographical organization is only as good as your knowledge of geography. Simple numerical order often does not give you any meaningful hint as to what the document is about.

5 Geoff's spreadsheet.xls and !!index.doc are both valid names. The name HAR/4129/03/2.doc is only valid if you are trying to store a file named 2.doc in a sub-sub-sub-folder named HAR/4129/03. You cannot use unknown??.doc because the system will refuse to save the file (but you can use the question mark as a wildcard when searching for files or folders).

6 The asterisk is a substitute for zero or more unknown characters. The question mark is a substitute for a single character.

Self-assessment 3 on pages 67–8

1 Our definition of a database is a collection of records arranged to allow quick and easy identification of specific information.

2 Databases can be used for communication with customers (mail merge) to help maintain relationships; they can also help to identify new sales opportunities.

3 Out of this list only a library card index catalogue would be considered to be a database. A collection of training videos and a training manual do not count, though a directory of training videos or a catalogue of training manuals would.

4 It is easy to insert the wrong type of information in a field unless the field has some check mechanism that prevents it, for instance if it is set to accept only numerical information in a certain pattern.

Fields can be limited to the appropriate size for the data that is to go in them. In this case if you tried to insert 18 characters into a 15-character field, the last three characters would not be accepted.

5 You might have listed four of the following:

- in alphabetical order of surname and initials, as with a telephone directory;
- by alphabetical order of town, and then by surname;
- by postcode;
- by age of installation or the date when services were performed;
- by type of agreement or contract with the client.

6 The functions should produce the following answers:

- =SUM(A1:A4)   42
- =A1*B1   £24.00
- =A2/D2   4
- =E1*20   10
- =(As+A3)/E1   52

Self-assessment 4 on pages 90–1

1 Excessive heat can damage storage media and lead to data being lost.

2 Risks include:

- fire (and the effects of fire-fighting);
- insects or mice chewing cables (yes, it has happened more than once);
- dust or smoke;
- liquid, ranging from a very humid atmosphere up to a spillage of coffee;
- excessive heat;
- strong magnetic fields;
- electrical power surges;
- being dropped, and other physical shocks.

3 When you tell a computer to delete a file, the file manager system removes the address of the file from the disk, but not the actual data. The space occupied by the file is available for storing other files and will gradually be overwritten.

4 There are two basic approaches to combating viruses. One is to install virus protection software. The other is to have a vetting procedure for all electronic data entering the organization.

5 Data must be:

- fairly and lawfully processed;
- processed for limited purposes;
- adequate, relevant and not excessive;
- accurate;
- not kept longer than necessary;
- processed in accordance with individual's rights;
- secure;
- not transferred to countries that do not have adequate data protection laws.

6 Individuals have various rights including:

- the right to be informed of all the information held about them by an organization;
- the right to prevent the processing of their data for the purposes of direct marketing;
- the right to compensation if they can show that they have been caused damage by any contravention of the Act;
- the right to have any inaccurate data about them removed or corrected.

7 The Data Protection Act lists eight categories of sensitive data.

- The racial or ethnic origin of data subjects.
- Their political opinions.
- Their religious beliefs or other beliefs of a similar nature.
- Whether they are members of a trade union.

- Their physical or mental health or condition.
- Their sexual life.
- The commission or alleged commission by them of any offence.
- Any details of court proceedings or sentences against them.

5 Answers to activities

**Activity 12
on page 13**

Let's say a typical hanging file weighs 600 gm and is 1 cm thick. Allowing for variations in thickness and leaving a little room for manoeuvre, each drawer in a standard filing cabinet can take 50 such files.

Thus if Stately & Graceful's 100 supplier files were 'typical', they would go comfortably in a four-drawer cabinet, leaving two drawers completely free.

A typical grey steel cabinet (measuring H132 cm × W47 cm × D62 cm), would cost £180 according to an office equipment catalogue. Suspension files and fittings would cost around £30 for a pack of 50. This would mean another £60 to accommodate 100 files.

A single filing cabinet is easy enough to cope with, and the files would only weigh 60 kg (though this is more than you'd want to fall on top of you).

For a small organization, this doesn't sound too alarming but an organization with 10,000 such files would be facing a completely different situation. It would need 50 filing cabinets, costing £9,000. The suspension files, bought separately, would cost £6,000.

The files would weigh six tonnes (10,000 × 0.6 kg), with at least another tonne for the cabinets themselves. If placed side by side, the cabinets would stretch 23.5 metres. Each cabinet occupies floor space measuring 47 × 62 cm, or 0.29 square metres. If we triple this space to allow staff to move among them, that means a total of 0.29 × 3 × 50 = 43.50 square metres.

You may like to check out office rental costs per square metre in your area and calculate the annual cost.

**Activity 18
on pages 33–4**

	Folder	**Cross reference(s)**
1	Hydraulic presses (production, sales etc.)	See also folder(s): 3, 7
2	Computerized lathes (production, sales etc.)	See also folder(s): 4, 5

3   *NQV Systems plc – Hydraulic
   press contract (3/2004)*   See also folder(s): 1

4   *NQV Systems plc – Computerized
   lathe contract (8/2002)*   See also folder(s): 2

5   *NQV Systems plc – Computerized
   lathe contract (3/2006)*   See also folder(s): 2

6   Dumali, S – correspondence   See also folder(s): 3, 4, 5

7   Another Company Ltd – Hydraulic
   press contract (6/2005)   See also folder(s): 1

**Activity 21
on page 39**

All the documents are of the same type (emails) and they are typically organized into folders (Inbox, Sent Items) under headings such as 'From' (or 'To'), 'Subject', and 'Received' date (or 'Sent' date).

You can improve this basic system by adding your own sub-folders. For instance, all internal memos could be put in a different folder to emails received from customers, and the customer sub-folder could be further subdivided.

**Activity 30
on page 58**

The whole letter would appear as follows.

Mrs DWG Thomas
Flat 4
25 Bland Road
Shirley
Birmingham
B29 2AA

25 September 2003

Dear **MRS THOMAS**

With Winter approaching, we would like to offer you an extra maintenance check for your **HOTFYRE 2005 GAS BOILER**. This service, which is over and above your normal **GOLD STAR PLUS** service, is entirely free.

Our engineers will be working in the **BIRMINGHAM** area on Thursday 18 October. If you would like an engineer to call for your free maintenance check please give us a ring or visit our website and click on 'Winter Offers'.

We would strongly encourage you to take advantage of this offer. Winter is the time when most problems with central heating systems occur. Also, because demand is so high at this time of year, repairs can take longer, and be more expensive.

Please note that engineers will carry out minor repairs and adjustments on the spot for no charge. If more major faults are discovered they may be repaired under the terms of your **GOLD STAR PLUS** agreement.

Yours sincerely,

6 Answers to the quick quiz

Answer 1   Banking records should be kept for six years because this is what is required by the law (tax legislation, company law, and so on).

Answer 2   You should keep the email for as long as you need it: probably at least until the end of next week, or longer if you think it may need to be referred to again, for instance to help you plan your work in subsequent weeks.

Answer 3   True.

Answer 4   Currently hard disks offer the greatest capacity, but there may be something new by the time you read this.

Answer 5   Probably b, under the first letter of the full name, though systems vary.

Answer 6   Cross-referencing is useful when documents could be filed in several different places, usually because they refer to a variety of matters for some of which there is a separate file. Indexing is useful whenever the coding system alone does not give you enough information to locate the document in question, for instance if numerical codes are used.

Answer 7   c. The character > is not allowed in a computer file name. There may be problems opening the other files if no specific application is associated with the extensions .001 and .5tg, and the computer will have no idea what software to use to open the file 'daisy2', which has no extension, but that does not make the file names invalid.

Answer 8   This is usually True, assuming you can remember at least part of the name. Searching by contents is slower because the computer has to examine the entire file and because there are likely to be several files containing the text you specify.

Answer 9   Records are in rows and fields are in columns.

Answer 10   Mail merge saves you from having to address separate letters for each person you want to write a standard letter to, and it also allows further personalization, depending on what information you have on file about the individual addressee.

Answer 11   A spreadsheet's ability to sort and filter data is limited – typically you can only use a maximum of three criteria. A database management package will allow much more sophisticated searching, sorting and extraction of data.

Answer 12   Files accidentally deleted from a disk can often be recovered provided that it is only the address that is deleted and the data has not been overwritten.

Answer 13   The best way is to take a backup and store it on a separate storage medium kept in a different physical location – and make it a regular habit to do so.

Answer 14   c is the most secure. The best passwords have at least 8 characters and are a mixture of numbers and upper and lower-case letters. Short passwords are easier to crack than long passwords, simply because there are fewer options to try. Passwords such as 'letmein' are very well known and will be amongst the first things that someone trying to break into a system will try. Passwords than contain elements of the user's name like 'susanj' are easy to crack if the intruder knows something about the user.

Answer 15   False. The eight data protection principles mean that you should not transfer the data to an organization based in a country with inadequate data protection. If you happen to take the data with you, do not give it to anyone and bring it home again that is fine. As it happens the USA does have adequate protection, but you need not have known this.

7 Certificate

Completion of this certificate by an authorized person shows that you have worked through all the parts of this workbook and satisfactorily completed the assessments. The certificate provides a record of what you have done that may be used for exemptions or as evidence of prior learning against other nationally certificated qualifications.

superseries

Understanding Workplace Information Systems

....

has satisfactorily completed this workbook

Name of signatory ....

Position ....

Signature ....

Date ....

Official stamp

Pergamon
Flexible
Learning

Fifth Edition

superseries

FIFTH EDITION

Workbooks in the series:

For prices and availability please telephone our order helpline
or email

+44 (0) 1865 474010
directorders@elsevier.com